Lady Margaret Beaufort and Her Professors of Divinity at Cambridge

Three leading scholars examine one of the oldest professorships, the Lady Margaret's Chair of Divinity at Cambridge, plotting its development in the context of sixteenth- and seventeenth-century history. The current Lady Margaret's Professor, Graham Stanton, sets the scene with an introduction briefly considering theology at Cambridge before 1502 and the Professorship after 1649. In the two main chapters (delivered as lectures in March 2002 to celebrate the 500th anniversary of the Chair) Richard Rex – an authority on John Fisher, first holder of the Chair – deploys new evidence to propose changes in the list of early Professors (including the removal of Erasmus' name) and shows how their appointment and dismissal reflected the vagaries of the Reformation; and Patrick Collinson investigates how the Elizabethan and early Stuart Professors continued to be caught up in the religious and political turmoil of the times. There is a complete list of holders from 1502 to the present.

PATRICK COLLINSON is Regius Professor Emeritus of Modern History, University of Cambridge.

RICHARD REX is University Senior Lecturer in Church History at the Faculty of Divinity, University of Cambridge. He is also Director of Studies in History at Queens' College, Cambridge.

GRAHAM STANTON holds the current Lady Margaret's Professorship of Divinity at the University of Cambridge.

Lady Margaret Beaufort
By Rowland Lockey (*c.* 1565–1616)

By kind permission of the Master and Fellows of St John's College, Cambridge.

Rowland Lockey was a famous portrait painter in his day. His signed and dated portrait of Lady Margaret Beaufort is said by Grove's *Dictionary of Art* to be a copy of a much earlier work, and a routine piece of decorative painting typical of an ancestor-obsessed age. The painting was presented to St John's College by Julius Clippersby in 1598, the year it was painted.

PATRICK COLLINSON, RICHARD REX
AND GRAHAM STANTON

Lady Margaret Beaufort and Her Professors of Divinity at Cambridge
1502–1649

CAMBRIDGE
UNIVERSITY PRESS

CAMBRIDGE
UNIVERSITY PRESS

University Printing House, Cambridge CB2 8BS, United Kingdom

One Liberty Plaza, 20th Floor, New York, NY 10006, USA

477 Williamstown Road, Port Melbourne, VIC 3207, Australia

314-321, 3rd Floor, Plot 3, Splendor Forum, Jasola District Centre, New Delhi - 110025, India

79 Anson Road, #06-04/06, Singapore 079906

Cambridge University Press is part of the University of Cambridge.

It furthers the University's mission by disseminating knowledge in the pursuit of education, learning and research at the highest international levels of excellence.

www.cambridge.org
Information on this title: www.cambridge.org/9780521533102

First published 2003

A catalogue record for this publication is available from the British Library

Library of Congress Cataloging in Publication data
Collinson, Patrick.
Lady Margaret Beaufort and her Professors of Divinity at Cambridge: 1502–1649 / Patrick Collinson, Richard Rex, Graham Stanton.
p. cm.
Includes bibliographical references and index.
ISBN 0 521 53310 4 (pb.)
1. Theology – Study and teaching – England – Cambridge – History – 16th century. 2. Theology – Study and teaching – England – Cambridge – History – 17th century. 3. Beaufort, Margaret, Countess of Richmond and Derby, 1443–1509. 4. University of Cambridge – History – 16th century. 5. University of Cambridge – History – 17th century. I. Rex, Richard. II. Stanton, Richard. III. Title.
BT30.G7C65 2003
230′.07′3342659 – dc21 2002041705

ISBN 978-0-521-53310-2 Paperback

Contents

1
Introduction

GRAHAM STANTON

The importance of John Fisher's contribution to the University of Cambridge can hardly be exaggerated.[1] One historian even claims that 'at no other time has the university owed so much, for so long, to one man'.[2] His library was said to be the finest in England. He was highly respected as a learned scholar who encouraged the reception of humanist scholarship. It was Fisher who persuaded Erasmus to come to Cambridge and teach theology and Greek from 1511. Among

[1] I am grateful to my colleagues Dr Richard Rex and Dr David Thompson for advice on a number of points; all errors of fact and of judgement are my own.

[2] H. C. Porter, *Reformation and Reaction in Tudor Cambridge* (Cambridge, 1958), p. 3. In 1502 Fisher was elected University Chancellor, and was re-elected annually until 1514; from 1505 to 1508 he was also President of Queens' College. See C. N. L. Brooke, 'John Fisher as University Chancellor', in B. Bradshaw and E. Duffy (eds.), *Humanism, Reform and the Reformation Career of Bishop John Fisher* (Cambridge, 1989), pp. 47–66. For the history of the University, see the excellent bibliographies and helpful guidance in Elisabeth Leedham-Green, *A Concise History of the University of Cambridge* (Cambridge, 1996), pp. 247–57.

his many other considerable achievements was his successful encouragement of Lady Margaret Beaufort to establish a 'Professorship' in Divinity in 1502. He himself became the first holder of the post.

The lectures by Richard Rex and Patrick Collinson included here in expanded form were given on 1 March 2002 as the centrepiece in the Faculty of Divinity's celebrations to mark the 500th anniversary of the establishment of the Lady Margaret's Professorship in 1502. The special occasion was chaired by Sir Alec Broers, Vice-Chancellor of the University, who also presided at a gala dinner at St John's College the following evening. The College's fine portrait of Lady Margaret Beaufort looked out, as usual, over the dining hall. For this special occasion the dining hall was packed with present and former members of the Faculty of Divinity. What would Lady Margaret have made of the celebrations?

The distinguished historians Richard Rex and Patrick Collinson have no doubts about the importance of 1502. Their lectures tell the fascinating story of the establishment of the Professorship and the distinctive contributions of the early holders. But they do much more than that. They set the early history of the Professorship in its religious, political and social context. They both show not only how the early holders were caught up in the turmoils of the sixteenth and early seventeenth centuries, but the extent to which they contributed to the intellectual and theological ferment of their day.

Did Lady Margaret Beaufort intend her benefaction to lead to the renewal of the church or the University? Did she have in mind major changes in direction? Or were her initial hopes more limited? Those are difficult questions to answer. What is clear is that the establishment of the Professorship had consequences which neither Lady Margaret Beaufort nor John Fisher envisaged. But this is the fate of all major benefactors: if they are to make a lasting contribution to the institution they support, they must leave it free to develop as it will, for if their benefaction is tied up in knots, in due course it will wither away.

Richard Rex and Patrick Collinson tell the story from 1502 to 1649. The paragraphs which follow offer the merest sketch of 'before and after'. Perhaps the full story of the Lady Margaret's Professorship will be written one day. If so, it should be told with 'warts and all', for as we shall see, there have been some low points in the past 500 years, as well as times when the holders have made lasting contributions to theological scholarship, to the University, to the wider church, and to society.

In 1209 a group of scholars who had fled from Oxford in the wake of troubles there arrived in Cambridge. We do not know why they chose Cambridge as the site for the new scholarly community they established, but we do know why they left Oxford. With the consent of King John, the authorities in Oxford had acted in a heavy-handed manner in response to a mysterious death of a woman (perhaps a prostitute). The alleged murderer, who was a scholar, was not apprehended, but his associates were hanged in violation of the immunity expected. Some of the scholars who ran for their lives from Oxford to Cambridge were theologians.[3] So in all probability theology was taught from the very beginning. Indeed it is possible that the great polymath Robert Grosseteste lectured on theological topics in Cambridge in the 1190s, though there is no evidence for organised teaching of theology in the twelfth century.[4]

In about 1225 the Franciscans established a house in Cambridge, followed by the Dominicans by 1238. Along with other religious orders, their numbers and influence grew steadily. By the late fourteenth century three-quarters of Cambridge theologians were members of religious orders and theology dominated the University as a whole.

The fifteenth century brought several changes. The numbers of theologians declined somewhat, partly as a result of a drop in the numbers of the friars.[5] A negative reaction to Wycliffe's 'heresy' stifled creativity in theology for some time,

---

[3] See D. R. Leader, *A History of the University of Cambridge*, vol. I (Cambridge, 1988), pp. 17 and 33, where full references to the primary sources and the secondary authorities are given.

[4] Leedham-Green, *Concise History*, p. 4.

[5] See M. K. Jones and M. G. Underwood, *The King's Mother: Lady Margaret Beaufort, Countess of Richmond and Derby* (Cambridge, 1992), p. 203; Leedham-Green, *Concise History*, p. 19.

but recovery began around John Fisher's time at the very end of the century.[6] The traditional pattern of 'regency lectures', whereby recent graduates carried out most of the teaching without receiving a regular salary, was in decline, partly as a result of the increasing availability of printed books.[7] So it is not surprising that there were several stillborn attempts to establish salaried professors at Oxford. There is evidence that in Cambridge payment was made for some lectures, but 'they remained on an uncertain footing until an independent endowment could be found'.[8]

Towards the end of the fifteenth century Renaissance humanism began to change the intellectual climate, and by about 1500 the first stirrings were felt in Cambridge. But there was little impact on theology before Erasmus' arrival in 1511, and no sign of doctrinal upheavals until Luther's views began to make an impact in the 1520s.

Henry VIII's 1535 injunctions insisted that lectures should be on the Bible 'according to the true sense thereof and not after the manner of Scotus, etc.', and banned lecturing on Peter Lombard's *Sentences* which had long been the staple diet of theologians. Although this was a radical change, it is important to note that lectures on the Bible were not a new

[6] I owe the points made in this paragraph to Dr Richard Rex. See his *The Lollards* (Basingstoke, 2002).

[7] For full discussion, see Leader, *History*, pp. 242–63.

[8] Leader, *History*, p. 252.

development, for the Bible was studied in Cambridge in the preceding centuries. 'What humanists like More and Erasmus said about the blindness towards scripture in the Universities was directed against the methods used by scholastic commentators, the importance of scholastic disputation, and the ignorance of the Greek and Hebrew originals.'[9]

So neither the establishment of the Lady Margaret's Professorship in 1502 nor the arrival of Erasmus as a distinguished teacher of theology and Greek in 1511 is a watershed. However, both events accelerated changes which were already afoot, and both had a very considerable aftermath.

In chapter 3 of this booklet Patrick Collinson ends his story with Richard Holdsworth, the moderate Calvinist who was Lady Margaret's Professor from 1643 to 1649, the year of the execution of King Charles I. It is difficult to pin down the religious views of Holdsworth's successor, Richard Love, Professor from 1649 to 1661, but his appointment did not mark a radical change. In 1642 he preached an influential sermon critical of Laudianism and called for a greater emphasis on preaching, but he also defended bishops. In short, he was 'an adept survivor of the religious–political purges during the revolutionary years'.[10] At the restoration

[9] Leader, *History*, pp. 183–4.

[10] John Twigg, *The University of Cambridge and the English Revolution 1625–1688* (Woodbridge, 1990) p. 27; see also p. 117.

of the monarchy in 1660 Love insisted that his opposition to the revolutionary events of 1648–49 was well known; in order to continue to serve church and University, he had taken pains not to provoke the religious authorities to expel him.[11] Hence, as Master of Corpus and Lady Margaret's Professor, he was one of the few senior members of the University to retain his posts right through this turbulent period.

The restoration of the monarchy brought many radical changes of direction. Lady Margaret's Professors were not exempt. In 1660 Peter Gunning was appointed Master of Corpus and Lady Margaret's Professor by royal mandate. He had been a staunch royalist during the Interregnum, and had a reputation for militant opposition to nonconformity. However, his tenure of both posts was very brief: in 1661 'he was advanced to the more prestigious posts of Master of St John's and Regius Professor of Divinity'.[12] Gunning was clearly swimming with the tide!

In 1661 John Pearson was appointed to the Professorship, which he held until 1673. He was Gunning's close ally in the defence of episcopacy at the landmark Savoy Conference in 1661. He has been described as 'perhaps the most erudite

---

[11] Twigg, *Cambridge and the English Revolution*, p. 159.

[12] John Gascoigne, *Cambridge in the Age of the Enlightenment: Science, Religion and Politics from the Restoration to the French Revolution* (Cambridge, 1989), p. 31.

and profound divine of a learned and theological age'.[13] His *Exposition of the Creed* (1659) became an influential, widely used textbook.

Pearson made a major contribution to scholarship with the publication of his *Vindiciae Epistolarum S. Ignatii* (1672). The letters of Ignatius, with their strong emphasis on episcopacy, were written *c.* 100 AD. Not surprisingly, they were a bone of contention in the seventeenth century: anti-episcopalians vigorously rejected their authenticity by claiming that the manuscripts had been interpolated or forged at a later period. Pearson's scholarly defence of the seven letters won the day, though the controversy was reopened in the nineteenth century. In 1885 another Lady Margaret's Professor, J. B. Lightfoot, mounted what is still the classic defence of the authenticity of the seven letters.

Cambridge was rather ambivalent about the 'Glorious Revolution' of 1689. Humphrey Gower, Professor from 1688 to 1711, is a good illustration. Although he himself accepted the new order, he used his influence to protect his colleagues at St John's (where he was Master) who refused to take oaths of loyalty to the new monarchy. This involved 'some deft legal manoeuvring'.[14]

The eighteenth century is a sorry story both for the University and for the Professorship. Although John Newcombe

---

13 *The Oxford Dictionary of the Christian Church*, ed. F. L. Cross and E. A. Livingstone (Oxford, 3rd edn, 1997), p. 1245.

14 Gascoigne, *Cambridge in the Age of the Enlightenment*, p. 73.

held the Chair from 1727 to 1765, the longest tenure to date, he remained silent after giving his inaugural lecture. His successor, Zachary Brooke (1765–87), followed suit: 'in an obituary notice of him the professorship is described as a valuable sinecure which indeed it was'.[15] In 1788 the University urged the electors to the Chair to appoint someone who would lecture regularly in accordance with the regulations. John Mainwaring, who held the Chair from 1788 to 1807, made a promising start, but as soon as the numbers attending dwindled, he too ceased to lecture.[16]

How did this parlous state of affairs come about? Originally all University lectures were given in Latin. Although by the beginning of the eighteenth century most professors in Cambridge had abandoned this custom, the Lady Margaret's Professors were traditionalists. So it is not surprising that their lectures in Latin failed to attract an audience. And once this happened, they had a perfect excuse for not lecturing.

In 1809 Herbert Marsh (1757–1839) broke the spell of silence and lectured in English to large audiences of townsmen as well as gownsmen in the University Church. On his election to the see of Peterborough in 1819, however, he ceased to lecture, even though he retained his professorship until his death twenty years later.[17]

---

[15] D. A. Winstanley, *Unreformed Cambridge: A Study of Certain Aspects of the University in the Eighteenth Century* (Cambridge, 1935), p. 98.

[16] Winstanley, *Unreformed Cambridge*, p. 99.

[17] D. A. Winstanley, *Early Victorian Cambridge* (Cambridge, 1955), p. 175.

Marsh was an influential and controversial scholar and church leader. He was said by many to be the foremost bishop of his day, though this view was not unanimous. From Peterborough Marsh maintained a strong and reputedly aggressive influence in Cambridge. He refused to license clergy of Calvinist beliefs, and engaged in fierce controversy with Charles Simeon and the Evangelical leaders of his day. He was well known for his fierce opposition to the establishment of the Bible Society,[18] to hymns in services, and to Catholic emancipation. He was the last Lady Margaret's Professor to hold the Chair and a bishopric simultaneously.

Marsh was an important pioneer in scholarly study of the Gospels. He was the first scholar to claim that a narrative source and a sayings source were two major independent sources used by the synoptic evangelists, thus anticipating the twin pillars of almost all modern study of the Gospels: the priority of Mark's Gospel and a collection of sayings of Jesus shared by Matthew and Luke known as Q.[19] Marsh was strongly influenced by J. D. Michaelis, under whom he studied in Leipzig in 1785. He translated the fourth edition of Michaelis' pioneering *Introduction to the New Testament*, added many of his own notes, and at the end of volume III

---

[18] See Winstanley, *Early Victorian Cambridge*, pp. 19–20.

[19] For recent discussion of the significance of Marsh's work for scholarly study of the Gospels, see Stephen Hultgren, *Narrative Elements in the Double Tradition* (Berlin, 2002), pp. 4–9. See also W. R. Farmer, *The Synoptic Problem: A Critical Analysis* (New York and London, 1964), pp. 11–15 and 61.

included his own 'Dissertation on the Origin of Our Three First Canonical Gospels'. The publication of this translation in 1801 aroused a great controversy, for historical critical approaches to the Gospels and to the Bible generally were felt to threaten the very foundations of the church.

William Selwyn held the Chair from 1855 to 1875. He will always be honoured for his contribution to the Faculty of Divinity in Cambridge. He had declined an invitation to become the first bishop of New Zealand, thus opening the way for his younger brother George Augustus to take up this pioneering role in 1842 at the age of 33.[20] On his election to the Chair, William Selwyn immediately offered nearly half his salary to his rival for the post, Herbert Browne, who held the much more poorly paid Norrisian Professorship. When Browne became bishop of Ely in 1864, Selwyn transferred his benefaction to a fund to provide a new home for the Faculty of Divinity. Selwyn's annual gifts of £700 paid almost the whole cost of the Selwyn Divinity School, so named in his honour.[21] The new building, which was opened in 1879 opposite St John's College, served the Faculty well until its much

---

[20] See John H. Evans, *Churchman Militant: George Augustus Selwyn Bishop of New Zealand and Lichfield* (London, 1964), pp. 17–35. Selwyn College, Cambridge was erected by public subscription in memory of George Augustus Selwyn, and incorporated in 1882.

[21] Winstanley, *Early Victorian Cambridge*, p. 328 n.5. See also E. G. Rupp, 'A Cambridge Centenary: The Selwyn Divinity School 1879–1979', *Historical Journal* 24 (1981), 417–28. Rupp includes a delightful pen-portrait of William Selwyn on pp. 418–22.

larger successor on the Sidgwick site was opened in 2000. Selwyn's generosity contributed indirectly to the funding of the new building, hence it is entirely appropriate that a statue of him has pride of place in the foyer of the new building. His published work was not negligible, for it included an edition of the first four books of Origen's *Contra Celsum*.

Selwyn was succeeded by J. B. Lightfoot, arguably the greatest of the Lady Margaret's Professors over the past 500 years. He went up to Trinity College in 1847, where he became a Fellow in 1852. He held the Cambridge Hulsean Professorship from 1861 to 1875, and made a significant contribution to the University. His long and distinguished career in Cambridge culminated in his tenure of the Lady Margaret's Professorship from 1875 to 1879. Lightfoot left Cambridge somewhat reluctantly in 1879 to become bishop of Durham, a see he held with distinction until his death in 1889. None of Lightfoot's successors as Lady Margaret's Professor has matched his contribution to biblical scholarship, to University governance and to national church life. A splendid huge portrait hangs in the 'Lightfoot Room' in the new Faculty of Divinity building, as it did in the Selwyn Divinity School.

Along with B. F. Westcott (Regius Professor 1870–90) and F. J. A. Hort (Lady Margaret's Professor 1887–92), Lightfoot is widely considered to have been one of the finest nineteenth-century biblical scholars. This great trio of scholars certainly put Cambridge on the map as an international centre of excellence for biblical and theological scholarship for the first time since the late sixteenth century. Lightfoot's commentaries on St Paul's epistles and on the Apostolic Fathers are still widely used today and remain in print: their linguistic rigour, their careful attention to detail and their nuanced judgements are unrivalled. As an example of Lightfoot's continuing high standing as a scholar, I shall mention the view of Professor Tjitze Baarda of Amsterdam. Over many decades he has made a detailed study of over 160 commentaries on Paul's letter to the Galatians written in many languages in the past 1500 years or so. His favourite commentary? J. B. Lightfoot's, of course.

Lightfoot challenged some of the radical views of F. C. Baur and the Tübingen School on the dating of early Christian writings and on the development of earliest Christianity.[22] Although often portrayed as an opponent of F. C. Baur's claim that early Christianity was deeply divided into radical Pauline and conservative Petrine camps, Lightfoot's views were more nuanced. For he recognised that Paul was frequently engaged in a struggle with conservative Jewish Christians and insisted that 'the systematic hatred of St Paul

---

[22] See lectures (with bibliography) by C. K. Barrett, James D. G. Dunn, Martin Hengel and David M. Thompson in *The Lightfoot Centenary Lectures*, a special number of the *Durham University Journal* (1992); B. N. Kaye, 'Lightfoot and Baur on Early Christianity', *Novum Testamentum* 26 (1984), 193–224; F. J. A. Hort in *Dictionary of National Biography*, vol. XXXIII, ed. Sidney Lee (London, 1893), pp. 232–40.

is an important fact, which we are too apt to overlook, but without which the whole history of the Apostolic age will be misread and misunderstood'.[23]

F. J. A. Hort held the Chair from 1887 to 1892. He is less well known than Westcott and Lightfoot, but he was considered by a near contemporary to be 'more the pure scholar and critic than either of the other two... too conscious of the possibilities of error and the limitations of knowledge to reach the clear-cut and assured conclusions of Lightfoot; too much alive to the complexities of thought and the inadequacies of human speech to be as prolific and facile a writer as Westcott'.[24]

Hort devoted most of his scholarly energies to the critical edition of the Greek text of the New Testament which he published with Westcott in 1881. This text was the foundation of the Revised Version of the English Bible (1881–85). Hort classified the early Greek manuscripts of the New Testament writings into four groups according to their textual characteristics: the unreliable 'Syrian' fourth-century conflated text (which lies behind the 1611 AV/KJV translation), the 'western' text, the Alexandrian text, and the 'neutral' text (claimed as the most reliable). Although this way of tackling the textual variants in the manuscripts has been partly undermined by

---

23 *St Paul's Epistle to the Galatians* (London, 6th edn, 1880), p. 311.

24 I owe this quotation from A. M. Fairbairn to D. M. Thompson, 'Lightfoot as Victorian Churchman', *Durham University Journal* (1992), p. 12.

further research and especially by the discovery in the twentieth century of numerous early papyri, Hort is still highly regarded as one of the pioneers of textual criticism.

W. R. Inge held the Professorship from 1907 to 1911. His first major book was his Bampton lectures, *Christian Mysticism*.[25] Shortly after he left Cambridge to become dean of St Paul's, a post he held from 1911 to 1934, he became 'a newspaper personality... and was at once christened "the gloomy Dean" by the *Daily Mail*'.[26] There must have been times when he would gladly have returned from St Paul's to the quiet scholarly life he led in Cambridge.

Inge's most considerable academic achievement was his *The Philosophy of Plotinus*,[27] the fruit of many years' work. His attempt in this book and in other writings to marry Platonic and Christian thought influenced the thinking of many Anglicans in the first half of the twentieth century.

J. F. Bethune-Baker, Lady Margaret's Professor from 1911 to 1935, was a prolific writer who became widely known as a leading Modernist. His standard textbook, *An Introduction to the Early History of Christian Doctrine to the Time of Chalcedon*, was first published in 1903; it was reprinted twelve times, most

---

[25] W. R. Inge, *Christian Mysticism* (London, 1899).

[26] See the not uncritical appraisal by Sidney Dark in *Five Deans* (London, 1928), pp. 209–55; here 214–15. See also W. R. Matthews in *DNB 1951–60*, ed. E. T. Williams and H. M. Palmer (Oxford, 1971), pp. 529–32.

[27] W. R. Inge, *The Philosophy of Plotinus* (Gifford Lectures, 2 vols., London, 1918).

recently in 1962. Perhaps the success of this textbook over many decades explains in part why Bethune-Baker was able to make a generous bequest to the Faculty of Divinity. His generosity is still appreciated by members of the Faculty who are awarded grants for travel from the Bethune-Baker fund.

Bethune-Baker is also remembered in the Faculty today as the founder in 1922 of the flourishing 'D Society' for discussion of philosophical and systematic theology. He served as editor of the influential *Journal of Theological Studies* from 1903 to 1935, a remarkably long stint.[28]

F. S. Marsh, a distinguished Syriac specialist, held the Chair from 1935 to 1951.[29] While serving as a chaplain to the Armed Forces from 1916 to 1919 he received gas wounds from which he never fully recovered. His major publication was *The Book of the Holy Hierotheos*,[30] an immensely learned critical edition and translation of a set of sixth-century Syriac manuscripts which had been sorely neglected since their discovery a century earlier. 'Holy Hierotheos' was used as a 'Mystic's Guide' right up until the middle of the nineteenth century. Although Marsh did not publish extensively, he became widely recognised as one of the most learned biblical scholars of his time.

---

28 See also Henry Chadwick in *DNB 1951–60*, pp. 97–9.

29 For an account of his life and work, see *The Cambridge Review* 24 (April 1954), 386–8.

30 F. S. Marsh, *The Book of the Holy Hierotheos* (London, 1927).

Charles F. D. Moule (Lady Margaret's Professor from 1951 to 1976) taught many graduate students who now hold chairs or senior posts in New Testament Studies in universities and colleges in many countries. With typical modesty he describes his *An Idiom Book of New Testament Greek* (1953) as 'an attempt to provide a syntactical companion to the interpretation of the New Testament'; it is still a standard reference work both for experienced exegetes and for students. Perhaps his most influential books are his wide-ranging study of earliest Christianity, *The Birth of the New Testament*, and his *The Origin of Christology*.[31] The latter explores the lines of continuity and development between the thinking of Jesus and that of the early church. At the age of 94 he still writes learned and perceptive reviews for the *Journal of Theological Studies* and preaches regularly at his parish church.

The appointment of Moule's successor in 1976 attracted considerable media attention. Morna D. Hooker (Lady Margaret's Professor from 1976 to 1998) is a Methodist, the first non-Anglican since 1660 to hold the Professorship, and the first woman to hold a chair in Divinity at either Oxford or Cambridge. She is a founding Fellow of Robinson College and a New Testament scholar who has made many notable contributions to study of the Gospels and Paul's letters. Her

---

[31] C. F. D. Moule, *The Birth of the New Testament* (London, 1962; 3rd edn, 1981) and his *The Origin of Christology* (Cambridge, 1977).

commentary *The Gospel According to St Mark*[32] is widely considered to be the finest one-volume commentary on this Gospel available.

C. F. D. Moule, Morna Hooker and Graham Stanton (appointed in 1998) have all served as Presidents of Studiorum Novi Testamenti Societas, the international learned society for New Testament scholars. It is now a Faculty of Divinity convention that the Lady Margaret's Professorship is held by a New Testament scholar.

And the future? Lady Margaret Beaufort's endowment of this post 500 years ago has been eroded by inflation almost to vanishing point. So unless the Chair can be endowed in the coming years in a way which takes full account of the ravages of inflation, the future is by no means secure. In a world (and even a University) which seems increasingly to turn its back on tradition and history, Cambridge's oldest chair with its more than 500-year distinguished history will not necessarily survive in future competitions for limited financial resources. Where can we find a new Lady Margaret Beaufort who will have the wisdom to recognise that the humanities disciplines, and theological studies in particular, will always have a major contribution to make to the well-being of society?

[32] M. D. Hooker, *The Gospel According to St Mark* (London, 1991).

2
Lady Margaret Beaufort and her Professorship, 1502–1559

RICHARD REX

Lady Margaret Beaufort, Countess of Richmond and Derby, generally known in Henry VII's reign as the King's Mother, is a lady who needs little or no introduction in Cambridge, where her memory is kept alive not only by the professorship whose quincentenary we are gathered to celebrate, but by a continuous oral tradition which hands on from generation to generation the tale of her benevolence and patronage towards the entire University. That tale was first summed up in the memorial sermon delivered a month after her death by John Fisher, Chancellor of this University, and her spiritual director. He described Lady Margaret as 'she that ordeyned .ij. contynual reders in bothe the vnyuersytes to teche the holy dyuynyte of Ihesu, she that ordeyned prechers perpetuall to publysshe the doctrine & fayth of cryste Ihesu, she that buylded a college royall to the honour of the name of crist Ihesu, & left tyll her executours another to be buylded to mayntayn his fayth & doctryne'.[1]

[1] *The English Works of John Fisher*, ed. J. E. B. Mayor (London, 1876. Early English Text Society, extra series 27), p. 308.

What Fisher does not tell us, with becoming modesty, is the role he himself played in all this. Lady Margaret and John Fisher were a kind of double-act. Fisher was a Yorkshireman from Beverley who came to Cambridge in the 1480s and became a fellow of Michaelhouse (later subsumed into Trinity College) around 1490. It was while serving as Senior Proctor in the academic year 1494–95, on a business trip to the king's court at Greenwich, that Fisher first met the King's Mother, an event which changed the course of his life and the history of the University. Cambridge's close, and not always comfortable, relationship with the Tudor dynasty can be traced largely to this meeting.[2] Fisher's talents obviously impressed Lady Margaret, for he was recruited to her service, becoming in due course her spiritual director. In this capacity he fostered her theological interests, which extended to translating devotional writings into English.[3]

It is surely no coincidence that the first signs of Lady Margaret's plan to found theology lectureships at Oxford

---

[2] *Grace Book B, Part I, 1488–1511*, ed. Mary Bateson (Cambridge, 1903), p. 68. See also Michael K. Jones and Malcolm G. Underwood, *The King's Mother: Lady Margaret Beaufort, Countess of Richmond and Derby* (Cambridge, 1992), p. 205 and Maria Dowling, *Fisher of Men: A Life of John Fisher, 1469–1535* (Basingstoke, 1999), p. 10.

[3] *English Works of John Fisher*, p. 295. On Lady Margaret and her books see Jones and Underwood, *The King's Mother*, pp. 179–87. On her relationship with the University, see Malcolm G. Underwood, 'The Lady Margaret and Her Cambridge Connections', *Sixteenth Century Journal* 13, no. 1 (1982), 67–81.

and Cambridge came soon after she met Fisher. For in letters patent of 10 December 1496 (reiterated in letters of 1 March 1497), Henry VII licensed her to make permanent endowments to support these lectureships.[4] In fact, the process took quite some time. The founding deeds were not sealed until 8 September 1502. Here you must please allow me a brief excursus to shoot down a *canard* which has been flying around since these quincentenary celebrations were advertised. Some worried people have written in to tell us that the lectureship was actually founded in 1503, not in 1502. Their anxiety is not justified. Both the original indenture in the University Library and an official copy in the Close Rolls of Henry VII give the date as the Nativity of the Blessed Virgin in the eighteenth year of Henry VII's reign: namely, 8 September 1502.[5]

---

[4] See *Calendar of Patent Rolls . . . Henry VII. Vol. II. A.D. 1494–1509* (London, 1916), p. 79 for the later letters. The earlier letters are not calendared, but are mentioned in the opening words of the founding charter (see below, note 5). See also Jones and Underwood, *The King's Mother*, pp. 206–8.

[5] The original founding deed is held at the Cambridge University Library in the Cambridge University Archives (CUA) Luard 144. A printed version is found in *Endowments of the University of Cambridge*, ed. J. W. Clark (Cambridge, 1904), pp. 58–65 (for the date, see p. 65). See also *Calendar of the Close Rolls. Henry VII. Vol. II. 1500–1509* (London, 1963), no. 770, pp. 291–3, summarising a single indenture of 2 March 1506 which consolidated the various earlier deeds and indentures relating to Lady Margaret's foundations at Oxford and Cambridge. The error stems from C. H. Cooper, *Memoir of Margaret, Countess of Richmond and Derby* (Cambridge, 1874), p. 89. His

In the meantime, Lady Margaret began to fund lecturers at both Oxford and Cambridge out of current account expenditure – 'soft money', we might say today. The university accounts for 1498–99 include a payment of 6s 8d to Mr Fawne 'for expenses towards the King's Mother regarding the foundation of the lecture', and that same year saw payments to lecturers at both universities recorded in her household accounts.[6] (The first Cambridge lecturer was in fact a man named John Smith – about whom we know either next to nothing or an incredible amount, depending on how you look at it.) Among the reasons for the delay was University business of a more pressing nature. Town and gown were locked in internecine strife, and Lady Margaret was appointed mediator. It is an interesting commentary on the University's priorities that the accounts for the years around 1500 have but one or two entries about Lady Margaret's lecture, but are packed with payments for the letters, missions, bribes and sweeteners needed to defend the University's legal and fiscal privileges. These accounts make fascinating reading. Those of you who are aware of the problems we have been having with the front door of this otherwise excellent new building will not be surprised by the following entry from

---

mistake, easily enough made, was to add 18 to 1485 to make 1503 the 18th year of the reign. The 18th year actually ran from 22 Aug. 1502 to 21 Aug. 1503.

[6] *Grace Book B, Part I*, p. 120. Jones and Underwood, *The King's Mother*, p. 208.

the year 1500: 'For repair of the door at the new place made for the doctors of theology, and for three keys to it, 10d.'[7]

Despite his commitments in the service of the King's Mother, Fisher continued to play an active part in university life, and in 1501 was elected your predecessor, Mr Vice-Chancellor. When Henry VII appointed him Bishop of Rochester in 1504, the University promptly elected him Chancellor, a post to which he was continually re-elected until 1514, when, to save energy, he was re-elected for life.

Fisher did everything to justify the confidence which the University placed in him and his powerful connections. Then, as now, academic leadership consisted to a large extent of raising money, and he delivered the goods. Lady Margaret's benefactions to Cambridge began shortly after she met Fisher, and if at first Oxford shared in her generosity, her attention was soon focussed exclusively on Cambridge. Under Fisher's influence she followed her divinity lectureships at Oxford and Cambridge with a preachership here alone. She went on to found two new colleges here, Christ's and St John's. In later years Fisher was at some pains to

---

7 *Grace Book B, Part I*, p. 138: 'Item pro reparacione hostii ad locum nouiter factum pro doctoribus theologie et pro tribus clauibus ad idem x^{d}.' It is worth paying tribute here to the excellent work of Mr Edward Cullinan and Mr Colin Rice in designing and building the new premises of the Divinity Faculty. However, among the 'niggles' which invariably beset any new building, the locking and opening mechanisms of the front door have been liable to recurrent malfunction.

emphasise that the credit for founding St John's College belonged not to him but to Lady Margaret, an anxiety which itself reflects the common perception of his role, attested in numerous letters of thanks and offers of commemoration presented to him by the University and the grateful colleges.[8]

Like all great academic entrepreneurs Fisher was well connected, and exploited his connections ruthlessly. Shortly after he was elected President of Queens' College in April 1505, he secured a big favour for his new base. The richest man in England after the king, Edward Stafford, duke of Buckingham, was persuaded by Lady Margaret – his great-aunt – to make over to the college 30 acres of prime land in Essex.

---

[8] Cooper, *Memoir*, pp. 247 and 252, prints extracts from the 'Thin Red Book' in the St John's College Archives, which record Fisher's role in diverting Lady Margaret's patronage towards Cambridge. Cooper gives further references (p. 252) to similar comments in several other sources. To these we can add Richard Croke, who owed his position as lecturer in Greek at Cambridge (along with a fellowship at St John's College) to Fisher, and remarked in his inaugural lecture that Fisher had persuaded Lady Margaret to found both Christ's College and St John's. 'Cui enim duo illa collegia vestrae academiae clarissima lumina debetis? Christi inquam & divi Ioannis, nunquid Roffensi? qui tantos sumptus illustrissimae & pientissimae dominae in vestrum decus & ingens commodum persuasit.' See his *Orationes Richardi Croci duae* (Paris, 1520), sig. a5r. Fisher's anxiety that gratitude towards him as a fundraiser was overshadowing proper gratitude to his patroness as a benefactor is evident in his letter declining an offer from the University of exequies in his honour, on the grounds that Lady Margaret should have first place in their prayers (Hymers, *Funeral Sermon*, p. 210). I owe this reference to Malcolm Underwood.

His deed of gift explicitly acknowledges Lady Margaret's influence – behind which, in turn, we can surely see Fisher's.[9] The following years saw one of Fisher's greatest coups. He fixed royal visits to Cambridge in both 1506 and 1507, and on the latter occasion treated Henry VII to a shameless piece of oratorical flattery in the as yet unfinished chapel of King's College.[10] It achieved its objective. On top of £1850 he had already given, Henry VII was persuaded to bequeath £5000 for the completion of that chapel.[11] Over the next twenty years, Fisher's connections among the landed gentry of Yorkshire and the humanist churchmen of London brought a stream of benefactions to Christ's and St John's Colleges. Although canonised in 1935, St John Fisher has not yet been declared patron saint of any interest group or occupation. His companion in martyrdom, Thomas More, has recently been named the patron saint of politicians. There is something to be said for the suggestion that John Fisher should be declared the patron saint of another distinctively contemporary occupation – fundraisers.

Lady Margaret's foundation, then, came into formal existence on 8 September 1502. Here you will permit me another

---

9 Cambridge University Library, Queens' College Archives, QC Box 29, deed of 15 June 1505. See also Underwood, 'Lady Margaret and Her Cambridge Connections', pp. 74–5.

10 For the text of the oration, see J. Lewis, *The Life of Dr John Fisher*, ed. T. H. Turner (2 vols., London, 1855), vol. II, pp. 263–72.

11 Dowling, *Fisher of Men*, pp. 26–7. *The Will of King Henry VII* [ed. T. H. Astle] (London, 1775), pp. 27–8.

brief digression on terminology. The Tudor era was oblivious to the subtle class distinctions we have introduced between lecturers, readers and professors, and used all three terms indiscriminately. In English, the Lady Margaret incumbent was generally known as a 'Reader' throughout this period. It was only in the later seventeenth century that 'Professor' displaced it in university parlance.[12] But in deference to what is now a venerable tradition, as well as to our modern pedagogical hierarchy, I shall employ the strictly anachronistic term 'Professor' for the rest of this lecture. In Tudor times, of course, university teachers were called 'readers' or, in Latin, 'lectores', because their job consisted essentially of reading a text, commenting on it and explaining it as they went. And, as we can easily learn from examining medieval depictions of lecturers, the reason we still call a professorial post a 'chair' is that originally lecturers performed from a seated position.

Few established posts in this University's history can claim to have had a first incumbent more distinguished than John Fisher. It would be easy to spend the rest of this lecture on

---

[12] CUA CUR 39.1, item 4[2], is a certificate of 24 February 1663, confirming the appropriation of the rectory of Terrington to the University by James I for the support of 'ye Lady Margarets Professor in ye said University'. Item 6, dated 6 February 1674, also concerning Terrington, speaks likewise of 'the Lady Margarets Reader or Professor'. The earliest instance known to me is in T. Fuller, *The History of the University of Cambridge* (London, 1655), p. 124. This work is bound in with his *The Church-History of Britain* (London, 1656).

an examination of his contributions to early modern theology, but in order to leave time for his successors, it is best to renounce this task on the grounds that none of his surviving works dates from his time as Professor.[13] Suffice it to say that I doubt that any other professorship anywhere can boast that its original incumbent died a martyr's death. Having said that, I should add that being Lady Margaret's Professor in Tudor Cambridge was almost as dangerous as being Chancellor. It is well known that five of the eight Chancellors in the sixteenth century were beheaded for treason. The risks facing Lady Margaret's Professors included execution, exile, imprisonment in the Tower of London, kidnapping, rebellion, and piracy on the high seas.

Identifying Fisher's successors is rather more problematic. The canonical list of the early Professors which is generally received in the University is taken from the *Historical Register* published in 1917.[14] That publication was designed to slim down the bulky annual *Cambridge University Calendar* by relieving it of its historical content. The *Calendar* had been including that same list of professors since 1850,[15] and had

---

13 For consideration of Fisher's theology, see Richard Rex, *The Theology of John Fisher* (Cambridge, 1991).

14 *The Historical Register of the University of Cambridge*, ed. J. R. Tanner (Cambridge, 1917), pp. 71–4.

15 *The Cambridge University Calendar for the Year 1850* (Cambridge, 1850), p. 128. The last issue of the *Calendar* to include the list was that for 1913–14 (p. 756).

itself drawn the list from a compilation of documents concerning Lady Margaret and John Fisher published at the University Press in 1840 by J. Hymers.[16] This in turn was an expanded edition of a work published in 1708 by the late Stuart antiquary Thomas Baker. Baker had published Fisher's sermon on Lady Margaret with various additional materials, including 'A Catalogue of Lady Margaret's Professors at Cambridge'.[17] He offered his new list in modest terms as 'differing from our receiv'd Accounts', submitting it to 'further Enquiry and Examination'.[18] Nobody seems to have given it a second thought since. The rest of this talk is offered by way of further enquiry. For the fact is, to paraphrase the words of another Cambridge man, that Baker has not put in names which he ought to have done, and has put in names which he ought not to have done.

Thomas Cosyn is a somewhat dubious name. Baker cites no evidence for his serving as Lady Margaret's Professor.[19]

---

[16] *The Funeral Sermon of Margaret, Countess of Richmond and Derby . . . with Baker's Preface to the Same*, ed. J. Hymers (Cambridge, 1840), pp. 62–82.

[17] *The Funeral Sermon of Margaret, Countess of Richmond and Derby* (anonymously edited by Thomas Baker, London, 1708). See unnumbered pp. [lxiv–lxxxi] for the catalogue. Baker was improving on the list offered by Fuller (*History of the University of Cambridge*, p. 124).

[18] Baker, *Funeral Sermon*, p. [lxiv].

[19] Baker, *Funeral Sermon*, p. [lxv], following Fuller, *History of the University of Cambridge*, p. 124, as he does for the succeeding names of Erasmus, John Fawne and Thomas Ashley.

But no evidence for or against has come to light, so his name is left in the list with a question mark. With the third name, William Burgoyne, we are on solid ground, for in 1507 and 1508 he was granted dispensations from some of his university obligations on account of his professorial commitments.[20]

Unfortunately, there is no evidence to suggest, and there are strong reasons for doubting, that any of the three men whom Baker lists next, Desiderius Erasmus, John Fawne and Thomas Ashley, actually held the Professorship. Both John Fawne and Thomas Ashley were in fact serving as Lady Margaret's Preachers at the times that Baker makes them Professors: he seems simply to have confused the two posts.[21]

---

[20] *Grace Book Γ*, ed. W. G. Searle (Cambridge, 1908), pp. 58 and 67. Some amusement was occasioned at this point by the display of a photograph of a portrait of Burgoyne belonging to his college, Peterhouse. There is no doubt that the picture is meant to portray William Burgoyne. But it was early given the mistaken label 'Thomas Burgen' (his brother), together with a bogus coat of arms in the corner. Moreover, as the portrait was painted long after his death, the 'likeness' must be considered notional. However, the robes of a Tudor Doctor of Divinity are accurately depicted. I should like to thank Dr Roger Lovatt of Peterhouse for making a copy of the picture available for the lecture.

[21] For Ashley, see Cambridge University Archives, Collect. Admin. 9 ('The Great Black Parchment Book'), p. 270, for the registration of his election as Lady Margaret's Preacher on 3 March 1519. From Ashley onwards, the Lady Margaret's Preachers subscribed an oath to fulfil the obligations of the position. These original subscriptions survive, in an apparently unbroken series covering over forty years. The 'Great Black Parchment Book' contains

The only reference to Erasmus in any Cambridge records, and the only evidence Baker offers, is a grace in 1506 offering Erasmus a DD – an offer he never took up.[22] Moreover, there is plenty of evidence to show that what he really did here was to teach Greek – notably his letters from the years 1511–14, which incidentally complain about the reluctance of students to pay their fees![23] Finally, we should note that Erasmus, who

---

nineteen subscriptions from fifteen individuals over the period 1519–65 (pp. 270 and 279–81). As Fawne was named in the founding charter, there would be no need to record his appointment elsewhere, and he may well have been tacitly granted life tenure (he died in 1519, the year of Ashley's appointment) as a reward for his prominent role in the foundation of both the Professorship and the Preachership. He was certainly still Preacher in 1508–9, when he was dispensed from various duties on account of his frequent absence (*Grace Book Γ*, p. 75). I have the impression of having seen a reference to Fawne as Lady Margaret's Preacher in 1515, but I am unable to substantiate this!

22 *Grace Book Γ*, p. 46.

23 *Opus Epistolarum Des. Erasmi Roterodami*, ed. P. S. Allen *et al.* (12 vols., Oxford, 1906–58), no. 233, vol. I, pp. 472–3, to Andrea Ammonio, 16 October 1511, reports that he has been lecturing on the Greek grammar of Manuel Chrysoloras, and that he intends to move onto that of Theodore of Gaza (p. 473). For a complaint about stingy students, see his letter to Ammonio of 28 November 1511 (no. 282, vol. I, p. 542). Confirmation of Erasmus' employment in Cambridge can be obtained from the inaugural lecture of Richard Croke as lecturer in Greek. Referring to Erasmus, Croke observes that he was someone 'quem vos olim habuistis Graecarum literarum professorem, utinamque potuissetis retinere. Succedo in Erasmi locum; bone deus quam infra illum, et doctrina et fama.' See his *Orationes Richardi Croci duae* (Paris,

was nothing if not a name-dropper, never so much as hints that he ever lived off the bounty of such an illustrious person as Lady Margaret.[24] We must, I would argue, expunge the name of Erasmus from our catalogue.[25]

1520), sig. c4r. John Caius mentioned neither Erasmus when discussing the Lady Margaret's Professorship, nor the Lady Margaret's Professorship when discussing Erasmus. In his *Historiae Cantebrigiensis Academiae* (of 1574), he notes merely that Erasmus lectured in Greek, in which task he was succeeded by Croke. See *The Works of John Caius M.D.*, ed. John Venn (Cambridge, 1912), pp. 102–3. If there had been any oral tradition of Erasmus serving as Lady Margaret's Professor, Caius would certainly have recorded it, as his history of Cambridge is far from critical in its methodology.

[24] *Opus Epistolarum Erasmi*, no. 3036, vol. XI, pp. 189–93, dedication to Christoph von Stadion of his *Ecclesiastae Libri IV siue De Ratione Concionandi* (Basel, 1535). Erasmus alludes (pp. 191–2) to the work of Fisher and Lady Margaret at Cambridge without mentioning the Professorship at all – an omission doubly odd if he himself had held it.

[25] One or two passing references in Erasmus' correspondence have fuelled speculation about his tenure of the Lady Margaret's Professorship. But it should be noted that where, in his footnotes, P. S. Allen made connections with the professorship (*Opus Epistolarum Erasmi*, vol. I, pp. 472, 492, 542 and 569), he was seeking to explain the obscure references in Erasmus' letters in the light of what he erroneously believed to be the clearer evidence of his tenure. He invokes Le Neve, who was presumably following Baker, who had no evidence. See John Le Neve, *Fasti Ecclesiae Anglicanae*, ed. T. Duffus Hardy (3 vols., Oxford, 1854), vol. III, p. 654. In his letter to Ammonio of 16 October 1511, Erasmus suggested that he might soon undertake a theology lecture (vol. I, p. 473, 'fortassis et theologicam lecturam suscipiemus, nam id nunc agitur'). Allen linked this with his comment to Ammonio a month later that he was much occupied with interpreting Jerome (no. 245, 26

In fact, the Lady Margaret's Professor through the 1510s was probably still William Burgoyne. For he paid personal tithes on his lecturing income from 1506 to 1520–21.[26] The

November 1511, pp. 491–3, at p. 492, 'diuo Hieronymo debes imputare, quem interpretandum suscepi'), but 'interpretari' would be an odd verb to use for lecturing (Erasmus had used 'praelegere' about his Greek lectures), and the text seems to refer to his work towards the edition of Jerome which he published in 1516, which we know he worked on in Cambridge (see his letter to Servatius Rogerus of 8 July 1514, no. 296, vol. I, pp. 564–73, at p. 570). That same letter to Rogerus did say that Erasmus had spent several months in Cambridge teaching Greek and sacred letters (p. 569, 'docui Graecas et sacras litteras'), but this probably means that, after covering basic grammar, he continued by lecturing on a Greek patristic text, such as Basil on Isaiah, of which he was at this time considering making a translation for John Fisher, who was responsible for his being in Cambridge in the first place (Rex, *Theology of John Fisher*, p. 62). (When John Cheke was Regius Professor of Greek thirty years later, he lectured on patristic as well as classical texts.) Even if Erasmus did take up a theology lectureship, there is no reason to conclude that it was Lady Margaret's. For he was residing in Queens' College, which had two internal theology lectureships, one on the *Sentences* and one on the Bible (see below, note 30), and he might more easily have taken up the Bible lectureship in college than the University lectureship. The Bible lectureship does not figure in the accounts for the years 1508–15 (it reappears in 1515–16). Purely speculatively, one might imagine that for some of this time Erasmus performed this task in exchange for free board and lodging in Queens'. See Cambridge University Library, Queens' College Archives, QC Book 1, fols. 209v–210r, 220v–221r, 230v–231r, 238, 251, 260v, 270r and 282.

26 Peterhouse College Archives, Bursars' Rolls. Such entries exist for 1506–7, 1510–11, 1512–13, 1516–17, 1518–19 and 1520–21. These are all the rolls that

sum is always the same, 6s 8d, which suggests a fixed income (most lecturing income varied with the number of students attending). The first payment was in the year in which he is first recorded as Lady Margaret's Professor, and the last was in the year 1520–21 – and we know that another man held the job the following year.

Once we reach the 1520s we are able to show that Baker's list is not only inaccurate, but incomplete. There is not time today for me to take you through the full working of my research. Suffice it to say that the puzzle was this: Why are there only a handful of explicit references to the Lady Margaret's Professor in the University records for the first fifty years of the professorship?[27] The solution lay in one of the first

survive from the period 1506–21, which suggests that the tithe payments probably continued throughout those fifteen years. The tithe is explicitly recorded as levied upon his lecturing income in all these entries except that for 1510–11. The tithe is always 6s 8d, except in 1506–7, when it is 3s 4d. If tithes fell due at Easter, this would make sense, as at that point he would have received only half a year's stipend. However, neither the rolls for 1521–22 and 1522–23 nor those for any later years record any tithes from him, which suggests that he ceased lecturing in 1520 or 1521. One earlier tithe payment from William Burgoyne is recorded (10s in 1504–5), but with no detail about the income on which it was levied (it looks too large to have been on income from lecturing). See also T. A. Walker, *A Biographical Register of Peterhouse Men, Part I, 1284–1574* (Cambridge, 1927), p. 81.

27 There may have been a record of subscriptions for the Lady Margaret's Professors similar to that for the Lady Margaret's Preachers (see above, note 21). If so, it seems to have been lost at an early stage. This possibility

rules of detective work: follow the money. Lady Margaret's foundation was based neither in Oxford nor in Cambridge – perhaps to make sure neither institution hijacked the whole thing – but in Westminster Abbey. A visit to the abbey archives showed that responsibility for paying the lecturers rested with the abbot of Westminster. Filed away among thousands of papers are a couple of receipts from 1522, which show that payment of the stipend was made from some abbey property in Bassingbourne, handed over direct to the Professor by the property's local manager, Mr Anthony Malory Esquire.

The name on the receipts is the first new name I can introduce into the catalogue of the Lady Margaret's Professors, to make up for the handful I have unceremoniously ejected. It is Dr Humphrey Walkden or Walden, a fellow of Queens' College.[28] Dr Walkden was a man of some consequence in Cambridge. A friend of Erasmus, he is of most interest to us for the light he can cast upon what the Lady Margaret's Professors actually taught in the early years. You might think that, as a friend of Erasmus, he would have

---

would account for the fact that, in the seventeenth century, John Davenant's subscriptions as Lady Margaret's Professor in 1608 and 1610 appear in the list of Preachers (CUA Collect. Admin. 9, p. 281).

[28] Westminster Abbey Muniments (WAM) 4704 and 4705, dated 26 October 1522 and May 1522 respectively, receipts for £6 13s 4d each (each representing a half year's stipend, for the half years to Michaelmas and Easter respectively).

shifted the focus of the lecture from scholastic to scriptural theology. Yet although another of Erasmus' friends at Queens' College, Dr Henry Bullock, was lecturing in college on Matthew in the academic year 1516–17, using Erasmus' text and annotations,[29] his colleague Dr Walkden was a dedicated scholastic. College accounts show that Walkden was lecturing on Peter Lombard's *Sentences* (the basic textbook of scholastic theology) in the years around 1520 – indeed, he seems to have given up his college lectureship when he became Lady Margaret's Professor.[30] He had also given ordinary lectures on theology in the University. In the academic year 1519–20, he petitioned for a dispensation from some of his obligations on the grounds that the University had

---

[29] *Opus Epistolarum Erasmi*, no. 579, vol. II, pp. 555–6, from Henry Bullock, 1 May 1517.

[30] Cambridge University Library, Queens' College Archives, QC Book 1, fols. 289v–290r, has payments to 'M Bullok pro lectura biblie' and to 'M Vmfrido Walkden pro lectura sentenciarum' in 1516–17. QC Book 2 has similar payments for 1517–18 (fol. 1); 1518–19 (fol. 7: fol. 7r specifies that from Easter to Midsummer Walkden was lecturing on Thomas); 1519–20 (fol. 18); and 1520–21 (fol. 29). In 1521–22 Walkden is replaced by Mr Thomas Bownde (alias Buynd, Bynde, etc. fol. 38), who graduated BD that year (*Grace Book Γ*, p. 201). This date would fit perfectly with the hypothesis that Dr Walkden relinquished his college lectureship in order to take up the Lady Margaret's Professorship, for which he received payment for the academic year 1521–22. It also fits the hypothesis that Dr Walkden directly succeeded Dr Burgoyne, whose last tithe payment on income from lecturing was made in 1520–21 (see above, note 26).

asked him to lecture on Book IV of Duns Scotus in the Long Vacation, over and above his lectures in college. Adding in his preaching obligations for his own and another college, he sought some relief from burdens which, he claimed, were too much for one man.[31] (Many of us know just how he felt. It is reassuring to report that he was granted some relief.) It seems fair to conclude that he continued lecturing on the *Sentences* in his new post.

Humphrey Walkden died in 1523, and from then until 1532 it has not been possible to identify any Lady Margaret's Professors, although there may be one or two more lurking in the Westminster Abbey archives.[32] Our next sighting of the Professor comes in the following fascinating document, a record of the election for the post in 1534.

---

[31] *Grace Book Γ*, p. 185. This grace shows that in 1519–20 he was also lecturing on Scotus in college.

[32] It might be noted that during his Vice-Chancellorship (1529–30), Dr Buckmaster appointed a dozen theologians to attend a conference with Henry VIII to discuss issues such as censorship and the vernacular scriptures. See Corpus Christi College Library MS 242, fol. 18v. Among these twelve men were four DDs (John Watson, Eudo (or Guy) Wygan, Edward Crome and Geoffrey Downes) and four BDs (Nicholas Shaxton, Hugh Latimer, John Thyxtill and James Hutton). The four MAs (Mr Tylson, John Skip, Nicholas Heath and Ralph Bayne) were all studying theology, but had not yet proceeded to a higher degree. There is a good chance that one of the eight theology graduates was in fact the Lady Margaret's Professor – most probably Eudo Wygan, who in 1540 was appointed the first Regius Professor in Divinity.

> The Saturday in the same week [28 February 1534], in the Regent House, was at 10 o'clock, which was immediately after a dirge mass, the election of a new reader in Divinity, which was proclaimed in the Schools three days before to be at that time and place. First was ministered unto them the oath to choose a fit man, by Dr Buckmaster, Vicechancellor's deputy and Reader at that time. And in the head were Dr White and Dr Buckenham (the one as Vicechancellor, the other as oldest doctor), and also Mr Middleton, as oldest Bachelor in Divinity. First they wrote their own voices every one in a sundry piece of paper, and then likewise everyone beside gave up their voices unto the head, written with their own hands. And so Dr Buckmaster was chosen *unanimi consensu*, and so published by the oldest doctor. That done, Dr Buckmaster read over the foundation immediately from the beginning to the ending. The voices be given from the youngest bachelor to the oldest doctor. There were not past 11 or 12 voices given at that election.[33]

Not the least interesting implication of this record is that it shows the elections actually took place every two years, in accordance with the founding charter. Moreover, it also explains why the founding charter, in the University Library, is so tatty that it could not even be put in the display case for the little exhibition associated with this commemoration: the Professor literally had to read it out at the election, and

[33] *Grace Book A*, ed. S. M. Leathes (Cambridge, 1897), p. 230. I have modernised the spelling for clarity.

indeed he had to read it out every year in place of one mid-term lecture as well. Finally, it shows that Dr Buckmaster was originally elected Professor in 1532.

William Buckmaster was another prominent man around the University. A fellow of Peterhouse, he was Lady Margaret's Preacher from 1528 to 1530, and then Vice-Chancellor until 1531, before becoming Lady Margaret's Professor in 1532. He lived in exciting times. As Vice-Chancellor he oversaw a rowdy session in the Regent House in 1530 in which the University adjudged Henry VIII's marriage to Catherine of Aragon ungodly.[34] For this his reward was a royal grant transferring him to a more remunerative fellowship in King's Hall (now Trinity College), together with the privilege of holding with it benefices to the value of £100 a year.[35] Gratitude indeed. He was serving as Lady Margaret's Professor when Henry VIII broke away from the pope and set himself up as Supreme Head of the Church of England.

The Break with Rome changed the face of theology in Cambridge. Hitherto, Cambridge theologians had been quite clear about the place of the papacy. John Fisher had declared in 1521, in a sermon against Martin Luther: 'the heed

---

[34] Gerard B. Skelly, 'Henry VIII Consults the Universities of Oxford and Cambridge', in Guy Bedouelle and Patrick Le Gal (eds.), *Le 'divorce' du roi Henry VIII* (Geneva, 1987), pp. 59–75, at pp. 60–6.

[35] *A Catalogue of the Manuscripts Preserved in the Library of the University of Cambridge* (5 vols., Munich, 1980, facsimile reprint), vol. v, p. 232.

of the vnyuersall chirche *iure diuino* is the pope'.[36] It is inconceivable that the other early Lady Margaret's Professors would have disagreed. Indeed, Buckmaster himself was described in 1535 as 'of the old sort', that is, as one whose commitment to the Break with Rome was considered suspect, whose true sympathies were thought Catholic (although he duly took the oath to the royal supremacy), and whose replacement with more amenable spirits was advised. The particular occasion of change was the visitation of the university in 1535, conducted by agents of Thomas Cromwell, who had succeeded Fisher as the Chancellor of the University. (A visitation was a kind of early version of Teaching Quality Assessment, only the stakes were higher and the visitors were even more prescriptive.[37]) Cromwell's Injunctions for the University, promulgated that year by the visitors, prohibited lectures on Lombard's *Sentences* and stipulated that henceforth all theology lectures were to be on the scriptures. This was as much to do with politics as with theology and scholarship. For the injunctions also prohibited the study of canon

---

[36] *English Works of John Fisher*, p. 314.

[37] *Letters and Papers, Foreign and Domestic, of the Reign of Henry VIII*, ed. J. S. Brewer *et al.* (21 vols., London, 1862–1910), vol. IX, no. 661, John Ap Rhys to Cromwell, 22 October 1535 (for Buckmaster's old-fashioned views); and no. 666, 23 October 1535 (for his subscription to the supremacy). For the visitation, see F. D. Logan, 'The First Royal Visitation of the English Universities, 1535', *English Historical Review* 106 (1991), 861–88, esp. pp. 882–3.

law, and both scholastic theology and canon law embodied, and presumed, papal primacy within the church: a doctrine now redefined as treason.[38]

The new lecturing norms were to some extent represented in a series of lectures given in the academic year 1535–36 not by the Lady Margaret's Professor, but by the precursor of the Regius Professor in Divinity. The King's Readers were active in Oxford and Cambridge from 1535 until they were established as the Regius Professors in 1540. The first King's Reader at Cambridge was one Alexander Alesius, a friend of Cromwell's, a Scottish Lutheran who had taken refuge in England. His lectures were on the Psalms, and he wrote them up in a dedication copy for Henry VIII. The text was heavily indebted to Luther and Melanchthon, and uncompromising in its affirmation of the doctrine of justification by faith alone.[39] Alesius reports that his lectures aroused considerable hostility in the University. One suspects that native religious

---

[38] For the injunctions, see *Statuta Academiae Cantabrigiensis* (Cambridge, 1785), pp. 134–8.

[39] Gotthelf Wiedermann, *Der Reformator Alexander Alesius als Ausleger der Psalmen. Dissertation* (Erlangen, 1988), which includes a critical edition of the text. See also Richard Rex, 'The Early Impact of Reformation Theology at the University of Cambridge, 1521–1547', *Reformation and Renaissance Review* 2 (1999), 38–71, at pp. 64–7. One suspects that Thomas Cromwell had more tact than to forward Alesius' well-intentioned effort to the king, whose loathing for Luther was unmitigated despite his own break with Rome.

conservatism was intensified in this instance by xenophobia. In Tudor England, calling someone a Scot was *prima facie* grounds for an action for slander. And they didn't like Germans or heretics much either, so a renegade Scot teaching German heresy in Cambridge was always going to be batting on a sticky wicket.

The new style of scriptural lecturing was very probably put into practice by the next Lady Margaret's Professor, John Redman, one of mid-Tudor Cambridge's most prominent theologians.[40] More a humanist than a scholastic in his intellectual dispositions, and a man who enjoyed significant royal favour in the latter years of Henry's reign, he will

[40] Baker, *Funeral Sermon*, p. [lxv], refers to a receipt by Redman acknowledging payment of the Professor's stipend, dated 27 December 1538. It has not proven possible to trace this document (which may well since have disappeared), but when Baker makes claims as detailed and circumstantial as this, he is reliable. Assuming Baker is correct, then the instalment of his stipend which Redman received was probably that for the half year to Michaelmas 1538, in which case, as Buckmaster's appointment in 1534 would have expired in 1536, it looks as though Redman succeeded him that year and was reappointed for another two years in 1538. For a petition by Thomas Pylson to the king in 1539 seeking restoration to his fellowship at King's Hall, which he claimed to have resigned under undue pressure, states that he had originally secured it in November 1538 'by the helpe of hys singuler good Mr doctor Redmayn Reder of divinitie in the Scoles in Cambrige' (PRO E348/38), which suggests that Redman was still in post in the academic year 1538–39. (If Pylson had meant that Redman was the King's Reader, then he would probably have said 'Your Reader' in addressing the king.)

almost certainly have been implementing the new Injunctions by lecturing on the Bible. It was towards the end of John Redman's tenure that the post's future was brought into doubt by the suppression of Westminster Abbey in January 1540. Fortunately, Henry VIII was persuaded – quite possibly by Dr Redman – that the lecture was a deserving cause, and therefore authorised the resumption of payment, transferring liability to the Court of Augmentations, which had been set up in the 1530s to handle the proceeds of the dissolution of the monasteries.[41] It is from the excellent accounts kept by the Court of Augmentations that we are able to identify the Lady Margaret's Professors and Preachers for every year from 1542 to 1554. When you were handling the king's money, your accounts had to be proof against the most exact audit.

Payments of the Professor's stipend resumed in 1542, along with arrears to the current Professor for the previous year or so. These payments went to William Skete (or Skyte) of King's College.[42] As he was replaced by William Glyn, of Queens' College, from Michaelmas 1542, Skete himself had

---

41 A decree of the Court of Augmentations, dated 10 June 1542, and confirmed by letters patent of 26 June 1542, authorised the payments. The letters patent (which recite the decree in full) are in CUA Luard 164, and printed in *Endowments of the University of Cambridge*, pp. 73–5.

42 Court of Augmentations, Book of Payments 1542–43 (PRO E315/251), fol. 48v for payments on 16 July and 14 November 1542. The earlier payment was in respect of the whole year ending 25 March 1542. Skete took his BD in 1539 (*Grace Book Γ*, p. 337).

probably replaced Redman back in 1540. Of William Skete, I am sorry to report, we know next to nothing.

William Glyn, of Queens' College, and later a foundation fellow and first Vice-Master of Trinity, held the Chair from 1542 until 1549,[43] except for one year, 1545–46, when he was replaced, I presume for reasons of illness, by Simon Bridges of Pembroke.[44] Glyn resigned the professorship during the

---

[43] Court of Augmentations, Books of Payments 1543–44 (PRO E315/252), fol. XXXIIIIr (16 March and 25 November 1543); 1544–45 (PRO E315/253), fol. 30v (4 May and 20 October 1544); 1545–46 (PRO E315/254), fol. XXXVIIr (3 April and 13 October 1545); 1547–48 (PRO E315/256), fol. 39r (24 April and 3 October 1547); 1548–49 (PRO E315/257), fol. XXXVIr (6 April and 12 November 1548). In referring to these Books of Payments, it should be noted that the interaction of the accounting year (Annunciation to Annunciation) with the academic year (Michaelmas to Michaelmas) and the payment dates of the Professor's stipend (half-yearly in arrears after the Annunciation and Michaelmas) means that the payments recorded in, for example, the accounting year 1547–48 are made in respect of lectures given in the academic year 1546–47.

[44] Court of Augmentations, Books of Payments 1546–47 (PRO E315/255) fol. 52v, 'Symond Briges' (26 March and 30 October 1546). Of Bridges we know very little. A fellow of Pembroke, he graduated DD in 1547. He was appointed as a founding fellow of Trinity College in 1546, but it is doubted that he took up the place, as he seems not to have resided. See *Admissions to Trinity College, Cambridge*, ed. W. W. Rouse Ball and J. A. Venn (5 vols., London, 1911–16), vol. II, p. 1. He was employed as a royal commissioner visiting Canterbury and Winchester cathedrals in 1547. See W. H. Frere, *Visitation Articles and Injunctions of the Period of the Reformation* (3 vols., London, 1910), vol. II, pp. 146–50.

visitation of the University by royal commissioners (6 May to 4 July 1549), almost certainly under pressure – which may explain why the stipend owed him for his last year in post was actually paid to his successor![45] William Glyn's was the loudest voice of Catholic theology in Cambridge in Edward VI's reign. During the visitation, Glyn took the lead in defending Catholic doctrine on the eucharist in a series of theological disputations.[46] He handled his opponents so deftly that one of the visitors, Nicholas Ridley, who was supposed

[45] Hymers advanced the suggestion that Glyn resigned under pressure in his edition of Fisher's *Funeral Sermon*, p. 64. In my original lecture, I rejected his suggestion *tout court* because I had no clear evidence for it, and the Augmentations accounts suggest a simple chronological succession, with Glyn's tenure expiring in 1548 (see below, note 52, where his successor receives the stipend for the academic year 1548–49). However, Corpus Christi Library MS 106, p. 552 (red pencil pagination) transcribes a notice of 7 July 1549 for an election to fill the Lady Margaret's Professorship, vacant 'per cessionem venerabilis viri doctoris glyn'.

[46] The first disputation, on 20 June (Corpus Christi), was proposed by Dr William Madew (then Regius Professor of Divinity), with Dr Glyn leading the respondents. The second disputation, on 24 June (Nativity of John the Baptist), was proposed by Dr Glyn, which suggests that he was still Lady Margaret's Professor at this point, with Andrew Perne leading the respondents. The third disputation was on 25 June, with Perne proposing. See the diary of the visitation, Corpus Christi College Library MS 106, unnumbered leaves between pp. 490 and 491, printed in John Lamb (ed.), *A Collection of Letters, Statutes, and Other Documents* (London, 1838), pp. 109–20, at pp. 114–15.

to be the referee, kept on leaping into the ring to help out his candidates.[47] The visitors apparently decided to silence this tenacious champion, and at the end of the visitation the Vice-Chancellor announced that the Lady Margaret's Professorship was vacant.[48] Glyn left the University to become chaplain to the conservative bishop of Norwich, Thomas Thirlby, and under Queen Mary he was promoted bishop of Bangor, his native diocese. Perhaps the most revealing thing about Glyn, and one which casts much light on the early stages of the English Reformation, was his reply in Mary's reign, at the trial of the Protestant John Philpot, who charged him with hypocrisy for submitting in earlier reigns to religious settlements which went against his conscience. Glyn answered, 'I never liked your religion . . . I was the same manner of man then, that I am now, and a great many more. Marry, for fear we held our peace, and bare with that time.'[49]

It was for a long time thought that Glyn's resignation was followed by the re-election of John Redman to the

---

[47] John Foxe, *The Acts and Monuments* (8 vols., London, 1837–39), vol. VI, pp. 305–35, esp. 308–13 and 319–27. Glyn dealt especially sharply with a series of syllogisms advanced against him by James Pilkington (pp. 325–6). However, the diary of the visitation provides no direct evidence that the visitors silenced Glyn or that he was still Lady Margaret's Professor (though it records that on 27 June Ridley tried in vain to win over Glyn in a private interview – Lamb, *Collection of Letters*, p. 116).

[48] Lamb, *Collection of Letters*, p. 119.

[49] Foxe, *Acts and Monuments*, vol. VII, p. 668.

Professorship on Thursday 12 July 1549.[50] Baker's conjecture to this effect was based on the diary of the 1549 visitation of the University, which notes that on Sunday 7 July the Vice-Chancellor (William Bill) notified the University of an election the following Thursday. It also notes that on Monday 8 July 'D. Redmayne began his lector in the common scholes', and Baker seems to have jumped to the conclusion that Redman was lecturing as Lady Margaret's Professor – even though he could not have been elected until three days later.[51] In fact, the Augmentations accounts provide decisive evidence against Redman's re-election, as at no point is he recorded as receiving the stipend.

The man whom the Augmentations accounts record as having received the stipend for the years 1548–50 is the most surprising addition to the roster of Lady Margaret's Professors: John Cheke.[52] Cheke was one of Tudor England's

[50] Baker, *Funeral Sermon*, p. [lxv]. In fact, Thursday that week was 11 July 1549. This error derives from the transcript of the notice for the election (Corpus Christi College Library, MS 106, p. 552), which mistakenly gives the date as Thursday 12 July.

[51] Lamb, *Collection of Letters*, p. 119.

[52] Court of Augmentations, Books of Payments 1549–50 (PRO E315/258), fol. XXVIIv (4 July and 19 December 1549); 1550–51 (PRO E315/259), fol. 36r (7 May and 19 December 1550). His first payment is recorded on 4 July 1549, which may be an error, as the diary of the visitation has Cheke leaving Cambridge for Huntingdon that day in company with his wife (Lamb, *Collection of Letters*, p. 119). But a date in July 1549 would suggest that he

greatest scholars. Appointed the first Regius Professor of Greek when that chair was founded in 1540, he had been an assiduous lecturer, covering Sophocles, Euripedes, John Chrysostom and Maximus the Confessor. He had left around 1544 to become tutor to the young Edward VI, whose favour secured him election as Provost of King's College, Cambridge, in October 1548.[53] As the provostship was statutorily restricted to priests with a degree in theology, and the professorship clearly presumed the same qualifications, Cheke was not formally eligible for either position. But he

---

was the winner of the election scheduled for 11 July – and that he managed to claim the stipend for the academic year 1548–49, which should have gone to Glyn. Cheke's appointment seems to have caused some kind of difficulty with the payment of the stipend. The Vice-Chancellor's accounts for the academic year 1549–50 include an entry recording receipt of £16 13s 4d for the Lady Margaret's Professorship, a sum representing a year's stipend to 25 March 1550 with arrears (presumably for a quarter of the year). But there is no balancing expenditure! The Senior Proctor's accounts for that same year record costs of 6s for writing to London and Greenwich about securing the stipend of the theology lecture from Sir John Williams, the Treasurer of the Court of Augmentations. See CUA U.Ac.2 (1), University Audit Book 1545–1659, fols. 30v and 32v. I am unable to offer any explanation for these singular entries.

[53] King's College Ledger Book 1, fols. 338–340, registers the correspondence relating to Cheke's election as Provost, which seems to have taken place on 9 October (some letters date it VI Ides October, which is 10 October, but they are more likely to have miscalculated the Roman date than mistaken the standard date).

was exempted from the requirements at King's by an express royal mandate, and probably obtained the professorship on the same basis.[54] This gives him the distinction of having been the first layman to hold either position, let alone both. He was almost certainly the first layman ever to hold a university post in theology.

The identification of Cheke as the Lady Margaret's Professor enables us to attribute a document which has lain for centuries among the archives of St John's College. It is obviously a theology lecture, and apparently an inaugural lecture at that. Until recently it had been tentatively identified as the work of John Redman. However, the speaker, plainly a gifted Latin stylist, calls himself the head of a college, regrets his lack of qualification in theology, which he says he had to give up eight years ago just as he was embarking on it, and is eager to flaunt his ready access to the king's court and to boast of the years he has spent in 'the court of the king's children'. Of all the college heads in the 1540s, Cheke gives the best fit by far to this self-description. The lecture itself, an exposition of Psalm 119, verses 1–8, deserves fuller exposition than it can be accorded today.[55] It sets its author firmly on

[54] Edward VI's letter requiring his election as Provost and exempting him from the statutory obligations is copied in King's College Ledger Book 1, fol. 339r.

[55] St John's College, Cambridge, Archives, D107.3, fols. 235–57. In collaboration with Mr Malcolm Underwood, Archivist of St John's College, Cambridge, I am planning an edition of this short text.

the moralistic wing of the English Reformation. The rejection of popery, idolatry and superstition is accompanied by a biblical moralism rather than by a sense of evangelical liberation. It is, in short, typically English Protestantism. Cheke came to a tragic end. Fleeing the country for religious reasons in 1554, he was subsequently tracked down, kidnapped and brought back to England, where he recanted his Protestant beliefs. His death soon afterwards was put down to guilt and grief.

John Cheke's successor, receiving the salary from Michaelmas 1550 until late in 1553, was James Pilkington.[56] He is the only early Professor of whom we know for sure what he taught. For Martin Bucer, Regius Professor of Divinity when Pilkington was Lady Margaret's Professor, tells us that he was lecturing upon the Acts of the Apostles.[57] Pilkington in fact disputed against one of his predecessors in the chair, William Glyn, in the 1549 disputation on the eucharist which we have already mentioned.[58] His tenure of the post was curtailed by the accession of the Catholic Mary Tudor to the throne. Like many other leading English Protestants, Pilkington fled the country, eventually fetching up at Basel, where he lectured to the English refugee community in turn on

[56] Court of Augmentations, Books of Payments 1551–52 (PRO E315/260), fol. 26v (8 July and 3 December 1551); 1552–53 (E315/261), fol. XXVIIr (both 25 January 1553); 1553–54 (PRO E315/262), fol. XXVr (10 June and 24 December 1553).

[57] *The Works of James Pilkington*, p. ii.

[58] See above, notes 46 and 47.

Peter, Ecclesiastes and Galatians.[59] After his return he was appointed bishop of Durham, and in that capacity he published extensive English commentaries on the minor prophets Haggai (Aggaeus), Obadiah (Abdias) and Nehemiah.[60] The curse of the Lady Margaret's Professors, though, struck him too. Many years later, when he was bishop of Durham, a rebellion broke out among the Catholics of the North. They invaded his cathedral, burned the Book of Common Prayer, put up an altar and restored the mass. Bishop Pilkington disguised his daughters as beggarwomen and fled with them to London to escape the mob.

In 1554, the Court of Augmentations was wound up, and its responsibilities were transferred to the Exchequer. From this time, the Exchequer paid the various monies it owed Cambridge annually to the Vice-Chancellor, who was then responsible for distributing them correctly. Now that the University itself was handling the money, the Lady Margaret's Professors can be traced in the University's records and accounts.[61]

---

59 John Bale, *Scriptorum Illustrium Maioris Brytanniae Catalogus* (2 vols., Basel, 1557–59), vol. I, p. 741 and vol. II, p. 113.

60 Pilkington's commentaries can be found in *The Works of James Pilkington*, ed. J. Scholefield (Cambridge, 1842), where they are prefaced by a brief biography which forms the basis for my account.

61 CUA Luard 164, the letters patent exemplifying the decree of the Court of Augmentations regarding the payment of the Professor's stipend, is endorsed as having been enrolled in the Exchequer in the Michaelmas Term 1554.

Our last Professors are the two men who successively held the chair in the short reign of Mary Tudor: Thomas Sedgwick, Fellow of Trinity, and George Bullock, Master of St John's, both of whom were to play active parts in the restoration of Catholicism. Indeed, they were both involved in one of the most notorious episodes in Tudor Cambridge, the exhumation and burning of the bones of Martin Bucer during the visitation of the University in 1556–57 by the papal legate, Cardinal Pole.[62] Sedgwick had already made his doctrinal position clear in Edward's reign. Having assisted Glyn in the 1549 disputation on the eucharist, he led the Catholic team in a disputation against Martin Bucer in August 1550, arguing against Bucer's thesis that the scriptures alone and entire contain all that people need to know to be saved.[63] In Mary's reign, as Lady Margaret's Professor, Sedgwick was part of the 'away team' sent to represent Cambridge in the disputation with Cranmer, Latimer and Ridley at Oxford. Thomas Baker believed that Sedgwick vacated the Professorship in 1556, having seen in the Corpus Christi manuscripts

---

This was clearly the point at which the Exchequer formally took over the responsibility for the payment from the now defunct Court of Augmentations.

[62] For an account of the exhumation, see Martin Bucer, *Scripta Anglicana* (Basel, 1577), pp. 915–35 (at p. 926 for the involvement of Bullock and Sedgwick). See also Lamb, *Collection of Letters*, pp. 201–10 and 215–17.

[63] Foxe, *Acts and Monuments*, vol. VI, pp. 316–17 (1549) and 439 (Oxford). Bucer, *Scripta Anglicana*, pp. 717–32.

a notice for an election to the post in that year as Sedgwick's tenure was coming to an end.[64] However, the University accounts show that Sedgwick continued to draw the stipend in 1557 and 1558, so we can conclude that he was re-elected for a further two years.[65] Vacating his Professorship, he went on to replace John Young as Regius Professor in 1558. It was only at this point that George Bullock was elected Lady Margaret's Professor.[66]

John Mere's diary shows us that Sedgwick took his lecturing duties seriously, for on Wednesday 2 December 1556 the Vice-Chancellor seized an opportunity to address students in the Divinity Schools on a matter of perennial concern to university authorities: 'It. the Vic. was at the scholes agayne from viii to x, and betwyxte bothe the divinite lectures he had all

---

64 Corpus Christi College Library, MS 106, p. 468, transcribes a notice of 9 June 1556 for an election on Friday 12 June 1556 to fill the vacancy in the Professorship which has arisen 'per cessionem venerabilis viri doctoris Segeswyck'.

65 CUA U.Ac.2 (1), University Audit Book 1545–1659, fols. 55v, 58v, 63r and 67v record the payments to Dr Sedgwick for the years 1555–58. CUA CUR 39.1, items 2^1 (27 March 1555) and 2^2 (1555) are Sedgwick's receipts for half year stipends due at the Annunciation and Michaelmas respectively. These payments, which he received from the Senior Proctor, Mr Thomas Bayley, were probably the first made under the new arrangements with the Exchequer.

66 CUA U.Ac.2 (1), fol. 72v, records payment to Dr Bullock of £6 13s 4d, his half year's stipend to 25 March 1559. Although it does not specify that he is Lady Margaret's Professor, there was no other University post remunerated at that rate.

the regentes of the first and seconde yeres before hym beinge assisted with Drs Yonge and Segewyk and the proctors and moved and exhorted them to com to lectures.'[67] As Young was Regius Professor and Sedgwick was Lady Margaret's Professor, at least it is clear that the lectures were being provided.

It was the next visitation, by royal agents under Queen Elizabeth in July 1559, that brought the university careers of Bullock and Sedgwick to an abrupt end.[68] True to his name, Bullock did not go quietly. He sat tight in the Master's Lodge at St John's until the visitors came and required him to swear the oath to the royal supremacy. He refused, and was deprived of his mastership and his professorship. He never received the second instalment of his professorial stipend. At much the same time, Sedgwick lost his professorship, and also his fellowship at Trinity. Among the visitors, finding revenge doubly sweet, was none other than their predecessor, James Pilkington – who on 20 July succeeded both Bullock as Master of St John's and Sedgwick as Regius Professor.[69]

---

67 Lamb, *Collection of Letters*, p. 186. For another reference to Sedgwick's lecturing see p. 231 (14 May 1557).

68 The visitation began on 7 July 1559. See Thomas Baker, *History of the College of St John the Evangelist, Cambridge*, ed. J. E. B. Mayor (2 vols., Cambridge, 1869), vol. I, p. 146. The university gave the visitors dinner that day. See CUA U.Ac.2 (1), fol. 73r.

69 *Works of James Pilkington*, p. iii. For Queen Elizabeth's commission for the visitation of the university (20 June 1559), see H. Gee, *The Elizabethan Clergy*

Bullock and Sedgwick promptly took refuge in Durham, where Bullock was a canon of the cathedral. Eventually the visitors caught up with them there. Both men once more refused the oath of supremacy, Dr Bullock with trenchant words: 'he beleveth that the bisshope of Rome hath and ought to have the iurisdiction ecclesiasticall within this realme, and by playne and flate wordis he affirmed that the sea of that bisshope was the sea Apostolicke'. On 25 September 1559 Sedgwick was deprived of his vicarage of Gainsford, and Bullock lost his canonry in Durham cathedral.[70]

Sedgwick ended his days as an obscure Catholic recusant under strict orders not to stray outside 10 miles of Richmond in Yorkshire.[71] Bullock fled the country, as he had in fact done in the last years of Edward's reign.[72] It was at this point that

and the Settlement of Religion, 1558–1564 (Oxford, 1898), pp. 133–6. For the visitation articles implemented on this occasion, see Frere, *Visitation Articles and Injunctions*, vol. III, pp. 54–7. For Pilkington's admission as Master of St John's, see Baker, *History of the College of St John the Evangelist*, vol. I, p. 146. It is not clear whether Bullock's successor as Lady Margaret's Professor, Robert Beaumont, was appointed by the visitors or elected after the visitation. But he took up the post from Michaelmas 1559, and was paid the full annual stipend next year. See CUA U.Ac.2 (1), fol. 77v.

70 *The Royal Visitation of 1559: Act Book for the Northern Province*, ed. C. J. Kitching (Gateshead, 1975), pp. 21 (Sedgwick) and 25 (Bullock).

71 Gee, *Elizabethan Clergy*, p. 179.

72 *Matricule de l'Université de Louvain*, ed. A. Schillings *et al.* (10 vols., Louvain, 1903–67), notes Bullock's matriculation there in December 1552 and his return on 9 September 1568 (vol. IV, pp. 463 and 744).

his troubles really began. He lost whatever he had been able to take with him when his ship was boarded by pirates in the Channel, and he was unceremoniously dumped ashore in northern France. After spending a few years at the abbey of Ninove, in the Netherlands, he moved to Antwerp, where he died late in 1572, shortly after publishing his life's work, a biblical concordance.

For in his long exile, Bullock brought to completion what was possibly the biggest book ever produced by a Lady Margaret's Professor, the *Methodical Economy of Concordances of Holy Scripture*, published by Christopher Plantin in 1572. It is over 1300 pages long, and measures 40 cm in height, 25 cm in width, and 10 cm from cover to cover. Sadly, no scales were available in the library of St John's College, Cambridge, where I consulted this book, so it is not possible to give its weight. It is from the dedication of this work to Pope Gregory XIII that we learn most of the picturesque details of Bullock's career.[73] As with many of the things mentioned in this lecture, it would be possible to linger much more on

[73] George Bullock, *Oeconomia Methodica Concordantiarum Scripturae Sacrae* (Antwerp, 1572). The dedication to Gregory XIII is found at sigs. +3r–v, and the second dedication, to the Abbot of Ninove, at sigs. +4r–v. For a fascinating account of the financial details and difficulties of its publication, which the great printer of Antwerp, Christopher Plantin, undertook mainly as a prestige project, see Leon Voet, *The Plantin Press (1555–1589)* (6 vols., Amsterdam, 1980–83), vol. I, pp. 501–5. The Plantin archives also give us 1572 as the date of Bullock's death (not 1580 as was previously thought).

this breeze-block of a book. But time presses, and this little catalogue must end with George Bullock, the last Catholic incumbent of Lady Margaret's Professorship, in whom I detect a kindred spirit not simply as a papist but as a scholar. For he places himself not in the first rank of scholars, 'the innovators who first discover things useful in themselves to the human race' – such as for example, Mr Vice-Chancellor, pioneers in nanotechnology; nor yet in the second rank of those who 'exploit the discoveries of others or seek to add modifications of their own' – which is the most to which a theologian who believes in revelation can ever aspire; but in the third rank of those who 'take the discoveries or modifications of others and set them in a better order' – a good enough ambition for a mere historian. And I can only echo for my little effort the hope Bullock voices in his preface for his monumental work, namely that it will be 'not entirely unwelcome to scholars'.[74]

---

[74] *Oeconomia Methodica*, sig. ++1r.

I should like to record my special gratitude to Dr Peter Cunich, of the Department of History in the University of Hong Kong, for his invaluable assistance in navigating and interpreting the records of the Court of Augmentations, which were so important in correcting the early history of the professorship.

3
Some Lady Margaret's Professors, 1559–1649

PATRICK COLLINSON

Richard Rex has laid an excellent foundation and I must endeavour to erect on it a superstructure which will not be too flimsy, or too contrived, since a succession of Lady Margaret's Professors has no more natural coherence than a list of Regius Professors of Modern History, or of archbishops of Canterbury. What did Reginald Pole have in common with Thomas Cranmer, or Randall Davidson with William Temple? My title takes us from the mid-sixteenth century to the mid-seventeenth,[1] if only to get as far as one of the most admirable men ever to grace the chair, albeit in the most discouraging of circumstances, Richard Holdsworth. Along the way we shall meet ten other Professors: John Redman, Robert Beaumont, Matthew Hutton, John Whitgift, William Chaderton, Thomas Cartwright, John Still, Peter Baro, John Davenant and Samuel Ward; which will be to omit some.

---

[1] This is a somewhat extended version of a lecture given in the Faculty of Divinity on 1 March 2002. I acknowledge the substantial assistance of Dr Charles Knighton and Dr Ashley Null.

But before coming to the personalities we must attempt a small analysis of the fortunes of the Lady Margaret's Chair. The first thing to strike you about the list of Lady Margaret's Professors (as amended by Richard Rex) is that in the first hundred years of the chair there were twenty-one incumbents and in the second hundred years only nine; or, to alter our periodisation, eleven between 1542 and 1609 and three between 1609 and 1649.[2] There is no great mystery about this. The Chair was, strictly speaking, tenable on each election for only two years, and it is often referred to as the Lady Margaret Lectureship. (Present-day academics on their short-term contracts will not find the arrangements unfamiliar.) At first the Chair paid only 20 marks a year, later stabilised at a stipend of £10, although some holders of the Chair were in this respect more equal than others, Whitgift and perhaps Baro apparently being paid £20. The remuneration was a more complicated affair than the making out of an annual direct debit by the university treasurer, but I would prefer not to get into all that.[3] The Professors naturally needed something

---

[2] See Dr Rex's corrections to the list contained in J. R. Tanner, *The Historical Register of the University of Cambridge* (Cambridge, 1917).

[3] George Dyer, *The Privileges of the University of Cambridge* (Cambridge, 1824), pp. 103–4. For the parallel and if anything more complex history of the Lady Margaret Chair at Oxford, where the intention was to secure the professor an annual income of £20 (again, half that of the regius chair), see G. D. Duncan, 'Public Lectures and Professorial Chairs', in James McConica (ed.), *The History of the University of Oxford*, vol. III (Oxford, 1986), pp. 347–50.

more to make a living, particularly in view of the fact that, after 1559, many of them (but not Whitgift) were married men. So Robert Beaumont (1559–61) was Master of Trinity, Matthew Hutton (1561–62) Master of Pembroke, John Whitgift (1563–67) Master successively of Pembroke and Trinity: and so on. But John Still (1570–73) became Master of St John's (1574), and then of Trinity (1577), only after vacating the Chair. And there was some expectation of advancing to the Regius Chair of Divinity, which was worth £40. That happened to Hutton (Regius 1562–67), Chaderton (Regius 1569–80) and Whitgift (Regius 1567–69).

But the position of the Lady Margaret Chair was somewhat accidentally stabilised by the long tenure of the Frenchman Peter Baro, who lasted from 1574 to 1596.[4] Baro was an alien and had enough theological enemies to ensure that he could advance no higher, but enough friends to make sure that he and his large family should not starve. So his tenure was regularly renewed until, in 1596, *odium theologicum* found that his time was up. Not many years after that, James I augmented the stipend with the rectorial tithes of Terrington in Norfolk. So the Lady Margaret Chair became a living and perhaps a reasonably pleasant one, after,

[4] I owe a particular debt to Charles Knighton, who has shared with me his account of Baro, written for the *Oxford Dictionary of National Biography*. But for the careers of Baro's descendants, who settled in Boston, Lincolnshire, and King's Lynn, after a Peterhouse formation in three generations, see I. and J. A. Venn, *Alumni Cantabrigienses*, part I, i (Cambridge, 1922), p. 95.

in 1625, Mrs Alice Davers added the perk of 'a small garden in Cambridge'.[5] Oh, and you may like to know how many of the sixteenth- and early seventeenth-century Lady Margaret's Professors became bishops. I think the answer is five: Matthew Hutton, John Whitgift, William Chaderton, John Still and John Davenant. Am I right in thinking that Lightfoot, in the 1870s, was the last Lady Margaret bishop? They manage things differently in Oxford.[6]

These little lectures were intended to accompany a series of seminars in the Faculty of Divinity, which are separately published, on 'Scripture and Theology'. That theme is rarely absent from the academic careers of our chosen ten, and least of all from that of the first of them, John Redman, Lady Margaret's Professor from 1538 to 1542.[7] I am bound to speak with reverence of Redman, since he was not only the first Master of my college but its real rather than nominal founder, whose behind-the-scenes diplomacy at the court of the ageing and fast-degenerating Henry VIII and role as a royal commissioner not only brought about Trinity but probably saved other colleges from going the same way as the monasteries.

[5] Tanner, *The Historical Register*, p. 71.

[6] The implied reference is to Archbishop Rowan Williams.

[7] I rely for my account of Redman on Ashley Null's essay 'John Redman, the Gentle Ambler', which will appear in a collection on Westminster Abbey, edited by Charles Knighton; and, for Redman's contribution (to put it no higher) to the King's Book, on the work of C. D. C. Armstrong, so far unpublished.

But Redman is a deserving case for more than that. He was an attractive theologian who really ought to have his place in the new Anglican Calendar. The fact that as a leading Greek scholar he favoured the trendy new pronunciation (a shibboleth in Cambridge at the time) is enough to establish that he was not a dyed-in-the-wool conservative. But although the Anglicanism of later centuries had yet to be born or thought of, Redman was a theologian for Anglicans not only in the matter but in the manner, almost the manners, of his theology, a master of equipoise, but also a man of consistency in his intense moralism. As a leading authority has written: he 'attempted the middle way between the religious extremes of his day and won the respect of all concerned'.[8]

Thanks to Martin Luther, the point most at issue was justification and its relation to sanctification. Redman wrote a treatise on the subject *De Iustificatione*, and at about the same time contributed the relevant sections to the King's Book of 1543, which was supposed to define where the English church stood on these matters. Redman was an Augustinian but not a Lutheran. If salvation was all of grace, justification was not, as Luther had insisted, something imputed and brought about in an instant, through faith alone, and distinct from the process of sanctification. He wrote: 'Justification is not entirely conferred upon us in a single moment, as if there was no need of further growth in justice. On the contrary, the

---

[8] Null, 'John Redman'.

justified person in this life is in perpetual need of growth in justification.' Redman insisted that this, rather than Luther's perverted doctrine, was truly scriptural, the key being the reconciliation of Paul and James. This evidently pleased Henry VIII.[9] But within four years Henry was dead and in the new and Protestant dispensation Archbishop Cranmer taught justification by faith alone, and the traditional doctrine of the mass was denounced as idolatrous. Redman was awkwardly placed and would have been still more exposed if he had indeed resumed the Lady Margaret Chair in 1549, as the older authorities would have it, but which Dr Rex assures us he did not. Such was Redman's golden reputation that his last thoughts on the matters at issue, communicated as he lay dying at Westminster in October 1551, became a matter of public and prolonged controversy. According to the Protestants, he testified that the papacy was 'a sink of all evil' and masses for the dead were 'ungodly', and that he regretted that he had 'so much strived against justification by only faith'. While reluctant to discuss transubstantiation ('Jesus . . . will you ask me that?') he confessed that after researching the matter in the Fathers 'mine opinion that there should be transubstantiation . . . was quite dashed'. Naturally Catholics propagated

9 Richard Rex, 'The Early Impact of Reformation Theology at Cambridge University, 1521–1547', *Reformation and Renaissance Review* 2 (1999); *Ioannis Redmani Angli Sacrae Theologiae professoris de iustificatione opus* (Antwerp, 1555).

a different account of what was said, and in Mary's reign printed Redman's *De Iustificatione* as a true representation of the belief in which he had died. Our authority, Dr Ashley Null, concludes: 'In the end, Redman died too catholic on the chief article of protestant belief but too protestant on the chief articles of catholic belief.'[10]

Richard Rex has told us about the first two Protestant occupants of the Lady Margaret Chair, hitherto unknown in that connection: John Cheke (a sensational discovery on Rex's part), and James Pilkington, the first Protestant bishop of Durham. The Protestant succession continued with Robert Beaumont (1559–61), who, like Pilkington, had spent the reign of Mary in Zurich and, as Master of Trinity and Vice-Chancellor (from 1564–65 and 1566–67, dying in office), bore all the marks of a Marian exile and hot gospeller, which made him an uncomfortable enforcer of ecclesiastical uniformity at a time when Cambridge was seething with excited resentment of the royal policy of requiring the use of

---

[10] *A reporte of Maister Doctor Redmans answers to questions propounded him before his death concerning certaine poyntes of religion and now beyng with many in controversy* (London, 1551); John Redman, *A compendious treatise called the complaint of grace* (1556?); John Redman, *The complaint of grace. Printed in popish times, falsly and corruptly, many places being left out. Restored now, and those places put in out of a manuscript coppy. Out of the library of W. Crashawe* (London, 1609); *Original Letters Relative to the English Reformation*, ed. H. Robinson, vol. I (Cambridge, 1846), pp. 150–2; S. Stanton, *Some Masters of Trinity College* (Cambridge, 1898).

traditional, 'popish' attire, the surplice and square cap (or 'mortar board'), the beginnings of Elizabethan Puritanism. An early agitator in that cause, Thomas Wood, another returned exile and as a Leicestershire man Beaumont's fellow-countryman, reported that Beaumont had been 'very ernest at Cambridge about capp matters'; that he had turned back 'to the toyes of popery and pudles of superstition', and accused him of arrogance in riding in great state to Great St Mary's. Wood told a merry tale about the students cutting off the mane and tail of his horse while he was inside the church to make him 'a crown like a popishe prest'. Beaumont dismissed this tittle-tattle, assuring Anthony Gilby, the leading reformer in his own county: 'I ryde styll as homely . . . as ye have sene me ryde in Leicestershire.'[11] And indeed Beaumont's evangelical credentials should never have been in doubt. In his will he thanked God for calling him from 'the damnable pit of idolatry wherein I was plunged' and bringing him 'to the clear light of his glorious gospel'. 'And I protest that I will live and die in this faith which he hath given me.' At his burial he desired no 'popish ceremonies, or mistrustful prayers, as though my happy estate with God were doubtful'.[12]

[11] Patrick Collinson, *Godly People: Essays on English Protestantism and Puritanism* (London, 1983), pp. 106–7.

[12] C. H. Cooper and T. Cooper, *Athenae Cantabrigienses*, vol. I (Cambridge, 1858), p. 245.

But Beaumont's more tangible memorial is the remarkable collection of Tudor portraits with which he endowed his college and mine. In that same will, he bequeathed six pictures of 'our Founder, his parents and chyldren, to be set in the librarye as sone as it is buylded', directing that in the meantime they should be 'fairly and warily kept in the Master's Lodge'. And that is where Henry VII, Elizabeth of York, Edward VI and Mary are still to be found, with Elizabeth I (the portrait still there is not part of Beaumont's collection) apparently missing. In 1894 the massively statuesque portrait of Henry VIII was moved from the Lodge to the Hall, where it has presided over High Table ever since. All these portraits derive from Holbein's famous group portrait of the Tudors made for the Privy Chamber at Whitehall and destroyed by fire in 1627; while the Henry VIII is the only copy of Holbein's original which can be confidently attributed to a known artist, Hans Eworth. How such a royal collection came into the possession of this Leicestershire clergyman and academic is undocumented and unknown. Presumably it was after 1561, when Beaumont became Master of Trinity, a college with which he had no previous known connection. What that tells us about the mid-sixteenth-century art market in England I have no idea.[13]

---

[13] I owe my knowledge of this portion of Beaumont's will, and of the subsequent history of his collection of portraits, to Professor Simon Keynes of

Matthew Hutton (1561–63), who would end his days as archbishop of York, is not to be confused with his great, great, great grandson and namesake, the Matthew Hutton who was archbishop of York from 1747 to 1757, and briefly, for one year, archbishop of Canterbury: actually no risk of that, since I know rather less about the second Matthew Hutton than about picture dealing in the 1560s. Our Matthew Hutton was a decided Protestant and a very robust anti-Catholic, and he restores us to our theme of scripture and theology, or rather, the contested issue of the Bible and the church. The most dramatic moment in Hutton's Cambridge career came in 1564, when he was already Regius Professor, and in the context of Queen Elizabeth's famous visit to the University. The theological disputation staged for the queen's benefit addressed the proposition: 'Maior est scripturae quam ecclesiae authoritas' – Scriptural authority is greater than that of the church. Hutton was the proponent, and he not only stripped of all authority the historic church from which Protestants, on scriptural authority, had seceded, but denounced Rome as 'impudentissima meretrix', a shameless whore. His opponent was Andrew Perne, the notoriously tergiversationist Master of Peterhouse, who as Vice-Chancellor had presided under Mary over the burning of the bones of the Regius Professor, Martin Bucer, and as Vice-Chancellor again, under

Trinity College. And see now Xanthe Brooke and David Crombie, *Henry VIII Revealed: Holbein's Portrait and Its Legacy* (London, 2003).

Elizabeth, at Bucer's rehabilitation. Perne came close to calling Hutton a heretic when he objected that unless Hutton confessed the same fundamental articles of the faith which were retained and taught in the Roman church he deserved to be anathematised by all Christians. Not scripture but the church was the final court of appeal in all matters in controversy. 'Longe igitur antiquior est ecclesiae quam scripturae authoritas multoque sublimior', ecclesiastical authority older and more sublime. Cyprian had rightly called Rome the first of the churches. This cost Perne a bishopric and explains why he remained Master of Peterhouse and a dominant figure in Cambridge for another quarter century, to Cambridge's great advantage.[14]

Hutton insisted that Rome was a tottering ruin. 'Tempus ergo fuit ut exiremus ne ruina nos opporimeret' – time to get out before the ruins collapse on top of us. In the course of the debate Perne forced Hutton to admit that his description of Rome as meretricious had been a piece of wild rhetoric, thoughtlessly uttered, 'nimis inconsiderate'. But Hutton had

---

[14] A version of the Hutton–Perne disputation was edited by Nicholas Robinson, bishop of Bangor (d. 1585) and survives in Folger Shakespeare Library, MS V.a.176, fols. 69–77, with a copy by Thomas Baker in BL, MS Harley 7037, pp. 214–31. This is the source of the account of the royal visit in John Nichols, *The Progresses and Public Processions of Queen Elizabeth* (London, 1823), vol. I, pp. 151–89. See 'Perne the Turncoat: An Elizabethan Reputation', in my *Elizabethans* (London and New York, 2003), pp. 191–6.

not really changed his opinion. In a sermon preached in York as dean he again called the so-called 'holy Church of Rome' 'meretrix', 'the whore of Babylon'. Hutton was described by whoever published this sermon as 'a notable spirit', which may be something of an understatement.[15] He once had occasion to call his archbishop, Edwin Sandys, a papist, which he emphatically was not, producing the retort: 'Yf I be a papist, thow art a puritan.' Not surprisingly, Sandys told Lord Burghley, the prime minister of the day: 'I cannot live with that man.' Could he not be moved upstairs? 'The Bishopric of Litchfield would next serve the turn.'[16]

Hutton's successor as Lady Margaret's Professor, the future archbishop of Canterbury John Whitgift, shared his views on the status of the Roman church, and while he would not have expressed them as vigorously he did defend for his doctoral disputation the thesis that the pope is Antichrist, or so we are always told. However, Whitgift's own guns were to be pointed in another, opposite, direction, defending the church of the Elizabethan Settlement against the puritan demand for its further and more drastic reformation, which he did in an interminable controversy with the leading puritan ideologue, Thomas Cartwright, occupying three volumes of the Parker Society edition of his *Works*, these being virtually his only publications.

[15] Matthew Hutton, *A sermon preached at Yorke* (1579), Preface and fol. 2.

[16] Peter Lake, 'Matthew Hutton – A Puritan Bishop?', *History* 44 (1979), 189; BL, MS Add. 33207, fols. 5, 7, MS Lansdowne 50, no. 33, fol. 72.

So it may be logical if not chronological to take Thomas Cartwright, Whitgift's successor-but-one as Lady Margaret's Professor, first.[17] Cartwright was to earn such a legendary reputation in the annals of nonconformity that it is hard to sort out what was no more than legend from fact. We read that when he preached 'grave men ran like boys in the streets to get places in the Church'. I don't know when that last happened to the current incumbent of the Chair, Graham Stanton. Was it really necessary to take down the windows of Great St Mary's church to accommodate all who wanted to hear him, which may be no more than an old trope?[18] But the wide support he enjoyed from within the University when Whitgift, in the name of the University, set out to destroy him, even from future hard-line anti-puritans like Richard Bancroft, suggests that he did indeed possess charisma. Cartwright's first course of lectures as Lady Margaret's Professor had been on the early chapters of Acts, and they were employed to explore the scriptural platform for the ecclesiology we know as Presbyterianism: ministerial parity in place of hierarchy; the supposedly scriptural ministry of pastors, doctors, elders and deacons instead of bishops.

Two years later two young and hotheaded London preachers published, clandestinely, a manifesto called *An*

---

[17] A. F. Scott Pearson, *Thomas Cartwright and Elizabethan Puritanism 1535–1603* (Cambridge, 1925). But I have updated Cartwright's biography in the *Oxford Dictionary of National Biography*, forthcoming, 2004.

[18] Scott Pearson, *Thomas Cartwright*, pp. 23–4.

admonition to the Parliament which set out the same stall in racier terms. 'We in England are so far off from having a church rightly reformed, according to the prescript of Gods word, that as yet we are not come to the outward face of the same.'[19] Although he was urged by responsible men not to do so, since that would be to prolong a nine days' wonder, Whitgift decided, from whatever motives, that the *Admonition* had to be confuted.[20] When he published his *Answere to a certain libel intituled, An admonition*, it was Cartwright who responded, again from a secret press, with a *Replye*. By the time Whitgift had replied with *The defense of the answere*, to which Cartwright retaliated from foreign presses in *The second replie*, and even, God help us, *The rest of the second replie*, the Admonition Controversy had generated many hundreds of pages in which the fatal fault-line in the Reformed English church had been examined in exhaustive detail.[21] Was the

---

[19] *Puritan Manifestoes*, ed. W. H. Frere and C. E. Douglas (London, 1907, repr. 1954). But in the second edition 'not' was, significantly, altered to 'scarce', a correction made by hand in all surviving copies of the first edition (p. 9, n. 2).

[20] Patrick Collinson, *The Elizabethan Puritan Movement* (London and Berkeley, 1967; repr. Oxford, 1990), p. 121.

[21] The bulk of the 'Admonition Controversy', but lacking Cartwright's *A second replie* (Heidelberg, 1573) and *The rest of the second replie* (Basel, 1577), is contained in *The Works of John Whitgift*, 3 vols., ed. J. Ayre (Cambridge, 1851–53). There is an unsatisfactory digest in D. J. McGinn (ed.), *The Admonition Controversy* (New Brunswick, 1949). See Peter Lake, *Anglicans*

church bound to observe strictly scriptural norms in all that it taught and did, and especially in its polity? Cartwright insisted that it was, Whitgift that it wasn't, the establishment position which Richard Hooker would defend rather more dexterously twenty years later.[22] Whitgift's role in the Admonition Controversy laid down the ideological foundations for the campaign he would mount against puritan nonconformity as archbishop in the 1580s, which won him many brownie points with the queen, but few from anybody else.[23]

Anglican historians have habitually rubbished Cartwright's position as intellectually threadbare and indefensible. It wasn't, but here there is no space to explain why.[24] But something that Cartwright said to Whitgift may be quoted as indicative of the high-falutin' tone often adopted by Anglican apologists in addressing the issues which the Puritans raised: 'You in so often reproaching them . . . would make us believe

and Puritans? Presbyterian and English Conformist Thought from Whitgift to Hooker (London, 1988), chapter 1, 'What was the Admonition Controversy About?'

22 Amidst a vast literature, see especially some of the contributions to A. S. McGrade (ed.), *Richard Hooker and the Construction of Christian Community*, Medieval and Renaissance Texts and Studies 165 (Tempe, AZ, 1997).

23 Collinson, *The Elizabethan Puritan Movement*, part 5, '1584'.

24 M. C. C. Perrott, 'Richard Hooker and the Problem of Authority in the Content of the Elizabethan Church Controversies', unpublished Cambridge PhD thesis, 1996, chapter 3, 'The Authority of Scripture and the Necessity of Government: The Admonition Controversy of the 1570s', pp. 102–51.

that you are so notable a logician and philosopher as if logic and philosophy had been born with you and should die with you.'[25] Would Cartwright have said the same to Hooker? Probably and good on him, as they say in Australia, and perhaps in Graham Stanton's New Zealand.

What should be noted, as we pass on, is that the Cartwright affair was the occasion for the writing, by Whitgift and his patron Andrew Perne, of new statutes for the University, which were to remain in force until 1853. These converted Cambridge into a kind of Venetian oligarchy, with power taken away from the regent masters and vested in the heads of houses. The new statutes were first used, punitively, to deprive Cartwright of his chair, which sent him off to Geneva; and when he briefly resurfaced in Cambridge, Whitgift took away his Trinity fellowship, on the technical ground that he was in breach of the college statutes by failing to proceed to the priesthood.[26]

The tenures of the Lady Margaret Chair by Whitgift and Cartwright were punctuated by William Chaderton (1567–69), like Laurence Chaderton, the celebrated first Master of Emmanuel College, a Lancastrian, but only a remote relation.[27] Chaderton combined the staunch Protestantism

[25] Quoted, Lake, *Anglicans and Puritans?*, p. 15.

[26] Collinson, 'Perne the Turncoat', p. 197; Scott Pearson, *Thomas Cartwright*, pp. 29–44, 63–4.

[27] I am indebted to Dr Christopher Haigh for sharing with me his account of Bishop William Chaderton, written for the *Oxford Dictionary of National*

of a Matthew Hutton with prudent conformity, condemning the 'seditions, contentions and disquietude' aroused by Cartwright and other Cartwrightians and arousing the criticism of the outspoken Puritan Edward Dering as a mere time-server.[28] He was certainly a sedulous careerist who cultivated the greatest patrons of the day. If he owed the archdeaconry of York (1568) to the earl of Leicester (whose chaplain he was), who later advanced him to his first bishopric, Chester, it was William Cecil who made him President of Queens' (1569–79). In 1572 he petitioned Cecil, now Lord Burghley, for the deanery of Winchester, which would free him from 'the wearisome duty of lecturing',[29] but without success. Attempts to supplant Richard Cox as bishop of Ely also failed. But in 1579 Chaderton got his bishopric, the poorly endowed and burdensome see of Chester, where he made do by holding in commendam the wardenship of Manchester College and two rectories.

I did not intend in embarking on this thumb-nail sketch of Chaderton to make it quite so negative. He proved a

Biography (forthcoming, 2004). All details in what follows not otherwise referenced I owe to Dr Haigh.

[28] J. B. Mullinger, *The University of Cambridge*, vol. II (Cambridge, 1884), p. 215; John Strype, *Life of Archbishop Parker* (Oxford, 1821), vol. IV. According to the (old) *Dictionary of National Biography*, Chaderton took Cartwright's place as Lady Margaret lecturer, stepping back into his old chair, after his suspension.

[29] W. G. Searle, *History of Queens' College* (Cambridge, 1867, 1871), p. 308.

good and mostly successful bishop, an effective administrator, a preacher, and an encouragement to the minority of his clergy who were committed Protestant preachers. In 1595 he was translated to Lincoln, perhaps the reward for his vigorous efforts to deal with Lancashire's notorious Catholicism. Here too he proved that he understood the mentality, and the usefulness of godly preaching ministers afflicted with sensitive consciences where 'offensive' ceremonies were concerned. 'I will by the grace of God use all the best means I can devise by conference and brotherly exhortations with mildness and discretion to win them.'[30] Chaderton married his eight-year-old daughter to the ten-year-old son of a Cheshire gentleman, and the young couple lived with the bishop in Manchester until old enough to reaffirm their vows and set up house together. In one of his sermons Chaderton had notoriously compared marriage to groping for an eel in a barrel of snakes, which may explain why he fished his own child out of the barrel at such a tender age!

Thomas Cartwright was succeeded by John Still, harbinger of the new and highly plausible strategy, for those of a moderate puritan disposition, of hanging on to their essential godly credentials, and their preferments, eschewing actual nonconformity and, in Still's case, discouraging it. Still's appointment as Master of St John's was intended to defuse a dangerously explosive contest in the college between

[30] HMC, *Salisbury MSS (Hatfield Calendar)*, xvii (1938), 133.

Puritans and conformists.[31] As archdeacon of Sudbury in the very years when a highly organised Puritan movement was gelling in west Suffolk (1577–93) (an office he combined with the masterships first of St John's and then of Trinity), Still was no great inconvenience to the preaching, nonconformist ministry.[32] Yet in 1589 Still preached a parliament sermon which dismayed Presbyterian Puritans.[33] As bishop of Bath and Wells, Still was the very epigone of the 'Prelate as Pastor', delineated in a definitive study of the Jacobean

---

[31] John Strype, *The Life and Acts of John Whitgift*, 3 vols. (Oxford, 1822), vol. I, pp. 140–4.

[32] The archdeaconry of Sudbury is poorly documented for this period and Still is an elusive figure in Elizabethan Suffolk. But what is said here is a reasonable inference from the conspicuous absence of Still's name from the struggle between Bishop Edmund Freke of Norwich and the Puritans of west Suffolk in the late seventies and early eighties. (See John Craig, *Reformation, Politics and Polemics: The Growth of Protestantism in East Anglian Market Towns 1500–1610* (Aldershot and Burlington, VT, 2001); and *Conferences and Combination Lectures in the Elizabethan Church: Dedham and Bury St Edmunds, 1582–1590*, ed. Patrick Collinson, John Craig and Brett Usher, Church of England Record Society 10 (Woodbridge, 2003).) But it is surely significant that the embattled parishioners of Bury St Edmunds in their dispute with the bishop over the appointment of their ministers were prepared to commit their 'interests of nomynacion' to Archdeacon Still and the doyen of Suffolk Puritans, John Knewstub. (BL, MS Egerton 1693, fol. 98r). In October 1578, Bishop Freke named Still among his 'adversaries' (PRO, SP 12/126/16).

[33] Matthew Sutcliffe, *An answere unto a certaine calumnious letter* (London, 1595), fol. 30v.

episcopate.[34] He got an excellent press from the wittiest of his Cambridge pupils, Sir John Harington ('to whom I never came but I grew more religious, and from whom I never went but I parted better instructed'), especially for the good that he did to Bath Abbey.[35] But Still might have been amused (or perhaps not) to learn that his modern biographers have spilt most ink over the question whether or not he wrote the raunchy comedy *Gammer Gurtons Needle*. Apparently he did not.[36]

Meanwhile the great, good and godly of Cambridge were finding it necessary, and perhaps convenient, to move away from controversial ecclesiological issues to defence of what they believed to be the doctrinal title-deeds of their church, the eternal decrees determining who would and who would not be saved, the theological construction usually labelled, somewhat misleadingly, as Calvinism.[37] It was necessary because these great teachers in Israel believed that the ark

---

[34] Kenneth Fincham, *Prelate as Pastor: The Episcopate of James I* (Oxford, 1990).

[35] Sir John Harington, *A Supplie or Addicion to the Catalogue of Bishopps to the Yeare 1608*, ed. R. H. Miller, Studia Humanitatis (Potomac, 1979).

[36] Sir Sidney Lee, writing in the *Dictionary of National Biography*. And see John Craig's article in the *Oxford Dictionary of National Biography* (forthcoming, 2004).

[37] Seán F. Hughes, 'The Problem of "Calvinism": English Theologies of Predestination *c.* 1580–1630', in *Belief and Practice in Reformation England: A Tribute to Patrick Collinson from His Students*, ed. C. Litzenbergen and S. Wasuda (Aldershot and Brookfield, VT, 1998), pp. 229–49.

of their covenant was in peril; convenient because it was safer for heads of houses like William Whitaker of St John's and Laurence Chaderton, the first Master of Emmanuel, to spill print on to the page in attacking Catholics and so-called 'Lutherans', Protestants who undermined or diluted the doctrine of predestinate election, than to continue the Cartwrightian attack on episcopacy, although they may have remained closet Presbyterians.[38]

Enter Peter Baro. Baro was French, and originally a lawyer, but in 1560 he was ordained in Geneva by Calvin himself. He came to England as an asylum seeker in the aftermath of the St Bartholomew massacre of 1572 and it was Burghley, as Chancellor of the University, together with Andrew Perne, who found him some support in Peterhouse (where, however, unlike his son, grandson and great-grandson, he was never a fellow) and, in 1574, secured for him the Lady Margaret's Professorship. Baro soon made clear his divergence from the strictest Calvinist orthodoxy in the direction of what would later come to be known as Arminianism, particularly in his lectures on the Prophet Jonah, always a favourite scripture for those who allowed human free will some part in the appropriation of divine grace, as well as in rejecting it. If Baro had been the late Frankie Howerd, he might well have complained: 'Infamy, infamy, they've all got it in for me!'

---

[38] Peter Lake, *Moderate Puritans and the Elizabethan Church* (Cambridge, 1982).

Whitaker, Chaderton, and Roger Goad, Provost of King's, originally a friend and patron, all had it in for him. He was, after all, an émigré and outsider, the Walter Ullmann and Geoffrey Elton of his day (although they both secured fellowships). The affair came to a head in 1595, when Whitaker denounced Baro's teachings in open congregation, and the relatively junior William Barrett, fellow of Caius and a front man for Baro, was hounded out of the University for a sermon which was a provocative apologia for the professor's views.[39] Why did Barrett choose to preach such a sermon in a university dominated by Calvinists? The only answer is the notice on the cage in the Jardin des Plantes. 'This animal is wicked. When attacked it defends itself.' However, when Chaderton interrogated Barrett on where he got his doctrine from, he allegedly admitted 'that he held the opinion of the Church of Rome', and certainly when he left Cambridge he converted to Catholicism, neither the first nor the last Caian to do so.[40]

The story of what followed is too long and complicated to be told on this occasion. Enough to say that the Cambridge disputes about grace, which were to be replicated all over Europe in the seventeenth century, not least in Catholic France, led to the drafting of the essentially Calvinist

[39] *Ibid.*, pp. 201–18.

[40] Sarah Bendall, Christopher Brooke and Patrick Collinson, *A History of Emmanuel College Cambridge* (Woodbridge, 1999), pp. 40–1.

Lambeth Articles of 1595, written by Whitaker but endorsed by Archbishop Whitgift, a kind of codicil to the Thirty-Nine Articles but repudiated by the queen and never given formal status, except in the Irish church. And, yes, Whitgift was a Calvinist, and so was Hutton, now his opposite number at York, who kept closely in touch with Whitgift throughout the affair, with nostalgic references to doctrines on which they were both agreed, back in their Cambridge days. As for poor Baro, he fought back in a university sermon which took the Lambeth Articles apart, and it was Whitgift who decided that he must go. Hutton had already told his brother that there were plenty of good men in Cambridge who could take Baro's place, and in 1596, when he was up for renewal, he was replaced by Thomas Playfere, and retired hurt to London, where he died little more than two years later.[41] Playfere was to the right of the Lambeth Articles, which is to say, a more pronounced Calvinist. I say 'poor Baro', because he appears in his published sermons not at all provocative (as Barrett had been) but open-minded and reasonable. He put the question: is man's will free or 'fettered with the necessity and bonds of Fate and Destinie?' 'At this day there is controversy touching this matter, not only betwixt the Romanists

---

[41] On Baro, Barrett and the Lambeth Articles, see the rather different accounts in H. C. Porter, *Reformation and Reaction in Tudor Cambridge* (Cambridge, 1958), pp. 344–75, and Lake, *Moderate Puritans*, pp. 218–42 (with Lake's to be preferred).

and the Protestants, but betwixt the Protestants themselves, and professors of the purer religion.' Could the matter be resolved? It appeared not. Then let both sides compromise a little.[42]

Thomas Playfere was one of James I's favourite preachers but he was a comparative nonentity, although when you next fetch a cake from Fitzbilly's you may like to inspect his charming funeral monument, complete with bust, in St Botolph's church.[43] Not so his successor, John Davenant, elected in 1609, we are told 'against seven competitors', who

---

[42] *Petri Baronis . . . in Jonam prophetam praelectiones 39* (London, 1580); Peter Baro, *A speciall treatise of Gods prouidence* (London, 1588?); *Fower sermons and two questions as they were uttered and disputed ad clerum in S. Maries church and schooles in Cambridge. By that learned Frenche man P. B. D. of Divinitye. And Englished by FL.* (London, 1588), esp. pp. 507 seq.

[43] See Peter E. McCullough, *Sermons at Court: Politics and Religion in Elizabethan and Jacobean Preaching* (Cambridge, 1998), pp. 117–18, 129, 130; and, for a copious sample of Playfere's divinity, *The whole sermons of that eloquent divine of famous memory: Thomas Playfere* (London, 1623). The collection includes *Nine sermons*, seven of which were preached before the king. In 1593, in a Paul's Cross sermon, Playfere enjoyed the benefit of forward sight. 'Glorious, gratious; It is our Crown and the highest ioy of our heart, that the Crowne of this kingdome is to bee set upon your royall head.' People 'runne and flocke together to behold and attend your Maiesty as some bright and beautiful starre, which by his divine sweete influence worketh a general prosperity and peace'. Like many of his colleagues, Playfere had occasion to complain of pirated versions of his sermons. 'I had rather have had my head broken, than my Sermons so mangled.'

continued in the Chair until 1621, when he was preferred to the bishopric of Salisbury. From 1614 Davenant was President of Queens', and, what is more to the point, in 1618 he was one of the five British delegates to a famous theological summit in the Netherlands, the Synod of Dort, which was staged to resolve the differences between the Arminian Remonstrants and Calvinist Contraremonstrants, but from the outset was loaded against the Arminians. We look forward to learning from Dr Anthony Milton what the British delegation got up to at Dort, when he publishes, quite soon, the relevant documents for the Church of England Record Society. But suffice it to say that the British delegates were all reckoned to be 'orthodox', and opposed to the Arminians, although they were careful to moderate their position, if only to disarm the opposition, particularly in their interpretation of the proposition that Christ died for all men, and on the thorny question of reprobation, so-called double predestination. That is to say, they were not what are sometimes called hyper-Calvinists.[44]

But Davenant's essential Calvinism is not in doubt. It is quite wrong to suppose, as Anglican historians used to, that the Lambeth Articles marked the end of the Calvinist ascendancy, the moment when the good old Church of England,

---

[44] Pending Milton's edition of the Dort documents, see his *Catholic and Reformed: The Roman and Protestant Churches in English Protestant Thought, 1600–1640* (Cambridge, 1995).

sound as a bell, recovered its marbles and became, well, Anglican. In fact the first two decades of the seventeenth century, an epoch of confessionalisation all over Reformation Europe, saw the confession we call Calvinism rampant, almost if not quite dominant in both Cambridge and Oxford.[45] In a dissertation on predestination and reprobation, Davenant asserted that election denoted that eternal act of the divine will which infallibly determined the salvation of certain persons; reprobation the 'oppositum actum' which decreed that certain other persons should be 'permitted' (the mark of a moderate Calvinism) to be excluded. And then follows a reminder that 'Calvinism' was much older than Calvin and should probably not be called that. 'Videte Aquinatem' – see Aquinas. Davenant's most famous work was an immense commentary on the Epistle to the Colossians, originally delivered as university lectures, which went through three editions between 1627 and 1639 and was thought to be worth reprinting, in translation, in 1831.[46] Davenant was the uncle of Thomas

[45] Nicholas Tyacke, *Anti-Calvinists: The Rise of English Arminianism c. 1590–1640* (2nd edn, Oxford, 1990).

[46] [John Davenant], *Determinationes quaestium quarundam theologicarum* (London, 1639); John Davenant, *Dissertationes duae: Prima de morte Christi . . . Altere de predestinatione et reprobatione* (London, 1650); John Davenant, *An exposition of the Epistle of St Paul to the Colossians* ('originally delivered in a series of lectures before the University'), trans. J. Allport, 2 vols. (London, 1831).

Fuller, the author of *The Worthies of England* and of much else besides.

Samuel Ward, who succeeded Davenant after an interregnum in 1623, and who remained Lady Margaret's Professor for twenty years, is someone we feel that we know, mainly because he has left behind an intimate diary, a typical puritan record of his ceaseless struggle to make good his calling against every temptation. Recurrent words are 'pride', 'negligence', 'slackness', 'unthankfulness'. 'Oh, what a wretch am I.'[47] There are reams of unpublished Ward papers in Sidney Sussex, to which he migrated from Emmanuel as Master in 1610. Through the 1620s and 1630s, as anti-Calvinist forces gathered strength in Cambridge and the church at large, Ward made himself the champion of what was becoming the good old cause, the sheet anchor of 'orthodoxy'. It was his misfortune to live on into interesting times, and as a royalist in parliamentarian Cambridge he died in custody in 1643, on the orders of Oliver Cromwell, who had been his student at Sidney. Davenant's nephew, Thomas Fuller, wrote of Ward: 'He turned with the Times as a Rock riseth with the Tide.'[48]

---

[47] Extracts, from the original in Sidney Sussex College, printed in *Two Elizabethan Puritan Diaries*, ed. M. M. Knappen (Chicago, 1933).

[48] Thomas Fuller, *The Worthies of England*, quoted in *Two Elizabethan Puritan Diaries*, ed. Knappen, p. 48.

I end with the most moderate of our Calvinist Professors, the ever admired teacher of an extreme anti-Calvinist, William Sancroft, the future archbishop of Canterbury. This was Richard Holdsworth, whom Sancroft called his 'card and compass', 'the gale that filled my sails'.[49] Holdsworth seems to have been beloved of all his pupils. When Simonds D'Ewes, his student at St John's, took him home to Suffolk, he preached 'so sweetly and profoundly' that D'Ewes 'began to love him even better than ever'. D'Ewes says that his sermons 'were by general approbation deemed extraordinary', and it is unfortunate that almost none survives in an incorrupt form. In 1637 Holdsworth was elected the fourth Master of Emmanuel, having been the victim of a stitch-up in his own college. But it was probably at St John's that he composed his famous 'Directions for Students in the Universitie', which help to explain why he was so popular.

Holdsworth shared with Samuel Ward the unhappy fate of a moderate caught up in the rapidly polarising conditions of a revolution. If the king and the parliament had managed to stick together in 1641, Holdsworth would have been part of the sticking plaster. He was one of five anti-Arminian moderates offered bishoprics as the revolution gathered pace, in October of that year, and he was the only one to refuse. He

[49] Bendall, Brooke and Collinson, *History of Emmanuel College*, pp. 73–5, 224–6; Patrick Collinson, article on Holdsworth in the *Oxford Dictionary of National Biography* (forthcoming, 2004).

had been in good odour with Parliament, but when the chips were down Holdsworth had to be a royalist. Most of the £100 Emmanuel contributed to the king's fighting fund came from his own pockets, and in March 1642, on the eve of the Civil War, he preached a robustly royalist sermon before Charles I in Great St Mary's, which, when printed by the university printer, caused great offence at Westminster. Parliament now reckoned him to be a malignant, and he was soon no longer a free agent. By June 1643 it was considered that he had forfeited his place as Master of Emmanuel. And it was at this point that Samuel Ward died, and that the University elected Holdsworth Lady Margaret's Professor in his place. This was taken to be a mere gesture and a provocation, and the new Professor was promptly imprisoned in the Tower. He never saw Cambridge or his books again (of the books he wrote: 'I would fain forget them but I cannot'). He died, still under restraint, in 1649, a little after the king's execution.[50]

His books! In the University Library I never write out a slip for an early printed book with the 'Syn[dicate]' classification without thinking of Holdsworth, for in 1664 his immense library of 10,000 volumes, after litigation over the terms of an unsatisfactory will (Emmanuel was the other interested party), found its way into the University Library. The terms of the judgement required the books to be kept apart from

[50] Bendall, Brooke and Collinson, *History of Emmanuel College*, pp. 243–6.

other books as 'Dr Holdsworth's Library'. But that didn't happen and now one can only assume that many of those 'Syn' books were originally Holdsworth's, without knowing which.[51]

Beginning with Redman and ending with Holdsworth, we seem to have come full circle. As deeply learned scholars and instinctively moderate theologians in a divided world, and above all as good men, these two would surely have understood each other very well.

---

[51] *Ibid.*, pp. 270–1.

APPENDIX I

Lady Margaret's Professors of Divinity at Cambridge, 1502–2002

Adapted from *The Historical Register at the University of Cambridge*, 1910, with later supplements.

Elected:

1502	John Fisher, Bishop of Rochester, 1504; President of Queens', 1505; Cardinal, 1535
1504	Thomas Cosyn, Master of Corpus; Chancellor of the University, 1490
1506	William Burgoine, Master of Peterhouse, 1518
1511	Desiderius Erasmus, Queens'
1515	John Fawne
1521	Thomas Ashley
1532	William Buckmaster
1538	John Redman
1542	William Skete
1544	William Glyn
1549	John Redman
1554	Thomas Sedgwick (or Segiswycke)
1556	George Bullock
1559	Robert Beaumont (or Beamond)

1561	Matthew Hutton, archbishop of York, 1596
1563	John Whitgift, archbishop of Canterbury, 1583
1567	William Chaderton (or Chatterton)
1569	Thomas Cartwright, ejected, 1570
1570	John Still
1573	John Hansome (Hanson)
1574	Peter Baro (or Barrowe)
1596	Thomas Playfere (or Playford)
1609	John Davenant
1623	Samuel Ward
1643	Richard Holdsworth
1649	Richard Love
1661	Peter Gunning
1661	John Pearson
1673	Ralph Widdrington
1688	Humphrey Gower
1711	Robert Jenkin
1727	John Newcome
1765	Zachary Brooke
1788	John Mainwaring
1807	Herbert Marsh, bishop of Llandaff, 1816; of Peterborough, 1819
1839	John James Blunt
1855	William Selwyn
1875	Joseph Barber Lightfoot, bishop of Durham, 1879
1879	Charles Anthony Swainson
1887	Fenton John Anthony Hort

1892 Joseph Rawson Lumby
1895 Arthur James Mason
1903 Alexander Francis Kirkpatrick
1907 William Ralph Inge
1911 James Bethune-Baker
1935 Fred Marsh
1951 Charles F. D. Moule
1976 Morna D. Hooker
1998 Graham N. Stanton

APPENDIX II

Lady Margaret's Professors of Divinity, 1498–1560

The University's list as revised by Richard Rex

Names in italics are conjectural. This list gives only the Professors' highest degrees and their most prestigious preferments in church, state and university.

Election or tenure

[1498*	John Smith (DD 1496; Vice-Chancellor, 1497–98, 1499–1500 and 1504–5)]
1502	John Fisher (DD 1501; Chancellor, 1504–35; President of Queens', 1505–8; bishop of Rochester, 1504–35)
1504	*Thomas Cosyn* (DD 1501; Master of Corpus Christi, 1487–1515)
1506	William Burgoyne (DD 1507; Master of Peterhouse, 1518–23)
1508–21	*William Burgoyne*
1521	Humphrey Walkden (DD 1520; Fellow of Queens', 1506–23; died 1523)

* In 1498 the professorship was as yet unestablished, and was financed from Lady Margaret Beaufort's household expenditure.

1532 William Buckmaster (DD 1528; Vice-Chancellor, 1529–30 and 1538–40)

1534 William Buckmaster

1536 *John Redman*

1538 John Redman (DD 1537; last Warden of King's Hall, 1542–46; first Master of Trinity, 1546–51)

1540 William Skete (BD 1539; fellow of King's, 1527–44)

1542–45 William Glyn (DD 1544; first Vice-Master of Trinity, 1546–51; President of Queens', 1553–57; Vice-Chancellor, 1554–55; bishop of Bangor, 1555–58)

1545–46 Simon Bridges (DD 1547; Fellow of Pembroke, *c.* 1537–46; appointed a founding fellow of Trinity in 1546)

1546 William Glyn (resigned 1549)

1549 John Cheke (MA 1533; Provost of King's, 1548–53; knight; privy councillor)

1550–53 James Pilkington (BD 1551; fled the country around New Year 1554; Master of St John's, 1559–61; Regius Professor of Divinity, 1559–61; bishop of Durham, 1561–76)

1554 Thomas Sedgwick (DD 1554; Vice-Master of Trinity, 1554–55; Regius Professor of Divinity, 1556–59)

1556 Thomas Sedgwick

1558 George Bullock (DD 1557; Master of St John's, 1554–59; deprived and fled the country, 1559)

1559 Robert Beaumont (DD 1564; Master of Trinity, 1561–67; Vice-Chancellor, 1564–65)

APPENDIX III

Benefactions of the Lady Margaret, 1502–1504

An extract from *Endowments of the University of Cambridge*, edited by John Willis Clark (Cambridge, 1904)

Readership or Professorship in Divinity

Margaret Beaufort, Countess of Richmond and Derby, mother of King Henry the Seventh, founded a Readership or Professorship in Divinity *(Lectura perpetua unius lectoris perpetui sacre theologie)*; and also a Preachership (*Cantaria perpetua unius predicatoris verbi dei*).[1] She obtained a license [*sic*] to found the former 10 December 1496, but did not complete the foundation until 1502, when by deed, dated 8 September, she declares the Readership to be established, prescribes statutes, and appoints John Fisher D. D., to be the first Reader. The licence to found the Preachership is dated 7 February, 1504, and her own deed of foundation 30 October, 1504, in which John Fawne, B. D., is nominated the first Preacher, and statutes are prescribed. The stipends

[1] See *Memoir of Margaret, Countess of Richmond and Derby.* By C. H. Cooper. Camb. 1874; and *Funeral Sermon of Margaret* [etc.] preached by Bishop Fisher in 1509. Ed. J. Hymers, B. D. Camb. 1840.

of both the Professor and the Preacher are to be paid by the Abbot of S. Peter's, Westminster, out of the revenues of certain lands conveyed to him by the Countess for that purpose. The deeds providing for these stipends are dated respectively 1 July, 1503, and 6 November, 1505. After the dissolution of the monastery both stipends were continued by decrees of the Court of Augmentations, confirmed by letters patent of King Henry the Eighth, dated respectively 26 June and 16 June, 1542.

King James the First, by letters patent, dated 6 August, 1605, granted to the University the Rectory of Terrington in Norfolk, for the augmentation of the revenue of the Lady Margaret's Professorship. This grant was not confirmed by Act of Parliament until the 10th year of the reign of Queen Anne (1711–12). It received the royal assent 22 May, 1712.

In 1625 Mrs Alice Davers, widow of Jeremy Davers, M. A., conveyed to Samuel Ward, D. D., then Lady Margaret's Reader, and to his successors for ever, a "garden, place, or parcel of ground" in S. Edward's parish, on the south side of Bene't Street, for reasons which are set forth at length in the conveyance.[2]

---

[2] Soon afterwards (1625) she surrendered to the University her interest in the house opposite, formerly Mere's, in order that the University might let it to the Lady Margaret's Reader. A lease of it for 99 years was accordingly granted to Samuel Ward, D. D. on the same day, in order, as the document

In 1856 an offer made by the Rev. William Selwyn, B. D., elected Reader 29 June, 1855, to give £700 a year to augment the salary of the Norrisian Professorship, so long as he and the then Norrisian Professor retained their offices, was accepted by Grace (14 May); and the principle was embodied in a statute which was accepted by Grace, 26 November, 1857. This statute, with a new statute for the Readership, was approved by the Queen in Council, 1 August, 1860.[3]

---

sets forth, that he 'and his successors Readers of the said Divinity Lecturers for the time being may be allwaies hereafter provided of a fitt and convenient house wherein he and they may inhabit and dwell during the time that he and they respectively shall continue to be Readers of the said Lectures'.

[3] *Statutes of the University*, 1896 edn, pp. 85, 86.

APPENDIX IV

The Lady Margaret's Professorship in 1824

An extract summarising the duties and responsibilities expected in the early nineteenth century (From George Dyer, *The Privileges of the University of Cambridge* (London, 1824), vol. I, p. 103)

1. Lady Margaret's Lecturer to read liberè, solenniter, et apertè such Books as the Vicechancellor & Doctors shall judge fittest, either from 7 to 8 in the Morning, or any other Hour at the Discretion of the Vicechancellor.
2. To read every accustomed Day in Term, except in Lent, & in the Long Vacation, to the 8th of Septemb. unless excused by the Vicechancellor for Infirmity or other just Cause.
3. Not to omitt his Lectures above 4 Daies in a Term, but upon just & reasonable Cause known and approved by the Vicechan. & the major Part of the Doctors in Divinity, & with Leave of the Vicechancellor.
4. Not to be absent on Pretence of such Leave above 14 Daies in a Term, & then to substitute a fit Person.

5. To be elected by the Vicechan. Doctors, & Batch[s]. of Divinity, under Oath of chusing the most worthy. On an Equality, the Vicechancellor to have the casting Vote. To continue 2 Years only.
6. To be admonish'd 3 Times for neglect of Duty or being guilty of any Ill in the Judgment of the Vicechan. & Doctors: if he offend after the third Admonition, to be deprived.
7. To read over this Foundation once a Year, instead of a Lecture: & to lose his Lecture in a Month, if he be Vicechancellor.
8. To swear at his Admission to observe these Orders: & to have for his Salary £13. 06*s*. 08*d*. yearly of the Abbot of Westm.

Lightning Source UK Ltd.
Milton Keynes UK
UKHW051456140119
335375UK00030B/716/P

9 780521 533102